Mob Rats - Jimmy "The Weasel" Fratianno

By Joe Bruno

Editor:

Lawrence Venturato

Published by:

Knickerbocker Publishing Company

Cover By: Alchemy Covers

Jimmy "The Weasel" Fratianno – He considered himself the quintessential "wiseguy," – "The Last Mafioso," like the title of his biography. But when Jimmy discovered there was a contract on his life, "The Weasel" became a bigtime "RAT."

On Friday November 18, 1977, the 64-year-old Aladena Jimmy "The Weasel" Fratianno knew what he had to do to save his life.

For the past year, after secretly testifying before a grand jury on a stock fraud case he had skillfully avoided taking part in, Jimmy had an ongoing conversation with FBI agent, Lowell "Larry" Lawrence. The two men frequently met in hotel rooms all over the West Coast and sometimes in Las Vegas, where they would chat about who-was-who and what-was-what concerning organized crime in America.

In Jimmy's mind, these were harmless meetings, where for more than a few bucks, Jimmy would tell Lawrence a little bit of this and a little bit of that, but never anything that could harm his pals in the mob. To Jimmy, he was performing the con on the feds, giving them useless information for money he could definitely use, since, between a wife who spent money like it was going out of style and Jimmy's love for three-legged horses, a man who made tens of millions of dollars in his criminal career, was almost flat broke. So far, Jimmy had tapped the feds for twenty grand, but if he were to turn canary bigtime, the feds better cough up some substantial cash, in addition to supporting Jimmy and his wife in the Witness Protection Program in the manner they had become accustomed to for the rest of their natural lives.

The turning point for Jimmy was the November 17, 1977 phone call from his best pal and top lieutenant, Mike Rizzitello (Mike Rizzi), who had once been a leg-breaker and bodyguard for "Crazy Joe" Gallo in Brooklyn. Jimmy had met Rizzi in late 1974, and was so enthralled with the Brooklynite's savvy and toughness, he insisted that West Coast mob boss, Dominick Brooklier (Brucceleri), make Rizzi a made man and then a captain, and then put him under Jimmy's wing. But since then Jimmy had fallen out of favor with Brooklier, and Jimmy knew if he was scheduled to get whacked, and now that was almost a certainty, no one could get close enough to put a slug in Jimmy's head, except for Mike Rizzi. Jimmy knew the rest of Brooklier's gang were useless and gutless, as was Brooklier himself. Brooklier was shrewd alright, but his next move was obvious to Jimmy. In fact, Jimmy knew this was the only card Brooklier had left to play.

When the kitchen wall phone rang, Jimmy let it ring five times before he answered. Standing next to Jimmy was his new flunky, Frank "Skinny" Velotta, who had been living with Jimmy for weeks, keeping Jimmy company while Jimmy waited for Brooklier to make his move.

"Yeah," Jimmy said.

"Hey, Jimmy, how have you been?" Rizzi said. "I haven't seen much of your lately. No one has."

"Yeah, and I'd like to keep it that way," Jimmy said. "So what's up? I'm busy with something."

"We've got to talk," Rizzi said.

"So talk," Jimmy said. "Who's stopping you?"

"No, this is important stuff. I can't discuss this on the phone," Rizzi said. "I'm at a phone booth in Los Angeles. Go to a pay phone right away. You know the one. I'll call you there."

"Mike, there's no fuckin' way I'm leaving the house tonight," Jimmy said. "Call me in a few days."

"This can't wait a few days."

"Then it's too fuckin' bad," Jimmy said.

"Okay, have it your way, Jimmy," Rizzi said.

"Fuck you, Mike!" Jimmy said.

And he banged the phone back into its cradle.

The next day, Jimmy "The Weasel" Fratianno learned from his contacts in the FBI, that Mike Rizzi had not been in Los Angeles the previous night, but, in fact, had been talking on a pay phone a quarter of a mile from Jimmy's house.

That cemented it for Jimmy. Now there was no turning back. It was time for Jimmy to tune up his vocal cords. The canary was ready to sing a sweet tune indeed.

Jimmy Fratianno was born on November 14, 1913 in a small town in the province of Salerno in Italy, near the city of Naples. From 1900-1915 three million Italian immigrated into the United States, 1913 being the record year for the influx of Italian into America. Most Italian men were laborers, and a select few were craftsmen. But most were poor when they were shuffled through Ellis Island and thrust into the mainstream of America.

When Jimmy was only four months old, his mother put them both on a ship to America to join Jimmy's father, Antonio, a laborer who had made the trip eight months earlier. They settled with relatives in Cleveland's Little Italy, also called "The Hill," which was situated in the Murray Hill/Mayfield Road section of Cleveland.

Like all Italian neighborhoods in America, the Italian Mafia had a big presence on The Hill, extorting money from their own kind in return for not breaking the poor Italian immigrant's arms and legs. One day when Jimmy was only six, he watched three men with machine guns make Swiss cheese of another man in front of Mafioso Tony Milano's speakeasy/brothel two blocks from Jimmy's home.

Little Jimmy was awed, but not frightened by what he had just witnessed. As his mother pulled Jimmy away from the bloodshed, all the kid could manage was an irreverent, "Holy mother of Jesus!"

Milano was a top "Black Hand" extortionist. They were called the Black Hand because they sent their victims threatening extortion letters with the imprint of a black hand on the bottom of the page. Tony's brother, Frank, was the boss of the local Mayfield Road Mob. The two brothers became Jimmy's role model in life, instead of a hard-working man like his father, who was an autocrat in his home and demanded fealty and obedience from Jimmy, his sister, Louise, and his brother, Warren. The fact that Jimmy was all too often on the opposite end of his father's whipping strap, made Jimmy a hard-case act in school; so much so, he demanded he be called Jimmy instead of his given name of Aladena, because, "Aladena sound like a broad's name."

After a few too many fights at the local Catholic school, Jimmy, at the age of nine, was sent to a school for wayward children, which his father coined the "bad boy school." One year living out of the home toughened Jimmy, but it also made him appreciate that hard work could translate into decent paydays.

When he returned home, Jimmy got a job hawking newspapers every night on the weekdays, and all day Saturday and Sunday. This impressed his father, Antonio, so much, that when Jimmy was eleven, he took his son under his wing and put him to work six days a week during Jimmy's summer vacation from school at the construction jobs Antonio was now supervising. The work was hard and exhausting, but the money was good, and Little Jimmy was enthralled with the things money could buy.

However, Jimmy also learned at the "bad boy school" that sometimes stealing, vegetables for instance, took less work than busting your hump to earn the money to buy those same vegetables. And that became Jimmy's side job – swiping vegetables from sidewalk stands. It was during one such adventure, that Jimmy earned his nickname for life.

Jimmy was considered the fastest runner of all the boys his age on The Hill. It was a piece of cake for Jimmy to sneak up on a vegetable, or fruit stand, snatch a few goodies, then sprint out of sight before the stand owner even knew what had happened. One day, just as Jimmy had grabbed a few tomatoes off a stand, a ruddy policeman of Irish descent took notice.

The cop yelled at Jimmy, "Hey, you! Give me back those tomatoes!"

And that Jimmy did, nailing the flatfoot between the eyes with a tomato that was more than slightly spoiled.

The policeman wiped his face and gave chase, but he was no match in foot speed for Jimmy.

As Jimmy dashed off into the distance, an old man yelled, "Hey, look at that weasel run!"

The cop stopped running and wrote the name of the perpetrator as "The Weasel."

Every time Jimmy was arrested on The Hill for stealing, which was often, the arrest report read "Jimmy 'The Weasel' Fratianno."

It would stay that way forever.

Jimmy's father lost hope his son would ever make an honest living, so to toughen Jimmy up, the senior Fratianno convinced Jimmy, if he wanted to be a tough guy, he must learn the proper way to fight with his fists. After a few weeks of training, including several miles a day of running up and down The Hill, Jimmy entered the Collingwood Community Center amateur boxing tournament. It's not clear if it was Jimmy's idea or not, but when Jimmy's hand was raised as the champion in the lightweight division, it was raised as "Kid Weasel."

During Prohibition, it was a natural progression for Jimmy to go from petty thief, to boxing champion, to waiter and bartender at "Bessie's Speakeasy." It was at Bessie's, that Jimmy met notorious gambler Johnny Martin, who taught Jimmy the tricks of the trade in cheating at poker with marked cards and shooting craps with loaded dice.

In no time, Jimmy was marking decks of playing cards like a pro. Using a pin or a sharp knife, Jimmy would put a system of tiny pinpricks, or slices on the back of special cards he wanted identified. If the card game contained more sophisticated players who would notice obvious marks on the back of the playing cards, Jimmy would use the block-out method, where he used a pen the same color ink used on the back of the card to slightly alter the designs.

But it was at dice that Jimmy made his big scores. Jimmy became an expert at palming the legit pair of dice while throwing the crooked ones, which Jimmy had doctored himself beforehand. Jimmy fixed the crooked dice by heating them on the stove, then cooling the dice, with the desired combination face-up (seven or eleven) during the cooling period (When hot dice cool, the bottom part of the dice gets heavier, causing the dice to falls face down on the heavier part).

By the time Jimmy was 17, he became Johnny Martin's partner in crooked games of chance held all over Cleveland, but not too often on The Hill, where being labeled a cheat could lead to serious bodily harm. Jimmy and Johnny were so good at what they did, they often cleared a few hundred dollars profit in a matter of hours. It didn't take a math genius to figured out this was easier work and a hell of a lot more profitable for Jimmy on an hourly basis than humping heavy concrete blocks at his father's construction site.

When Jimmy was 19, to meet the ladies he took to the local ice skating rinks. Jimmy was an expert and extremely fast skater, and the dolls just loved to see Jimmy do his thing on the ice. But their boyfriends were not too impressed.

One night Jimmy was showing off his ice skating moves at Elysium Park (later Cleveland Arena), at the corner Euclid Avenue and 107th Street, for the sake of a bevy of blonds, who just happened to be Polish. Suddenly, Jimmy was surrounded by five hulking Polacks, as Jimmy called them, and in seconds, the lights went out for Jimmy. Flat on his back, and trying to protect his face, Jimmy vaguely remembered getting the Polish Polka dancedd on his noggin. Besides being kicked in the side of the face by heavy boots, it was the vicious stomps directly on Jimmy's nose that caused the most damage.

After he awoke in the hospital, the doctors told Jimmy his nose was basically mush, and that it would take a series of operations to get his nose to approximately the same condition it was before the stomping. Jimmy told the docs to do what they could for now. And after the doctors tried to reconstruct his nose with grizzle from parts of his chest, Jimmy exited the hospital, and he neglected to ever go back for further plastic surgery.

Jimmy had more important things on his mind; like revenge.

Jimmy enlisted the help of his childhood friend, the 6-foot 200-pound Anthony "Tony Dope" Delsanter, the two men went on an expedition to right the wrongs done to Jimmy's face. Because Jimmy didn't know the names of his attackers, it took a while. But over the course of a year, Jimmy and Tony Dope caught four of them, one at a time. Using blackjacks and brass knuckles, the two Italians knocked their victims onto their backs. What followed next was an animated version of the Tarantella, aimed at the faces and the noses of the boys who had turned Jimmy's nose into silly putty. The fifth intended victim, hearing what had happened to four of his pals, did a lamsky to parts unknown.

Jimmy figured, four out of five ain't bad. So, Jimmy moved to his next scam, involving the trucking business, a venture in which Jimmy would make hundreds of thousands of dollars over the years; some of the money was even earned legitimately.

But not this time.

When Jimmy was twenty, he made the acquaintance of Jack Haffey, the district leader of the 26th Ward, which then encompassed The Hill. Haffey also worked as a state building inspector, and he told Jimmy that for a $500 kickback, Haffey would overestimate the contents of trucks delivering landfill to city projects. The city paid out 50 cents a yard of landfill, but when Jimmy's trucks were inspected by Haffey, he'd overestimate each haul by a yard, netting Jimmy an extra fifty cents over and above what his trucks would have made if Haffey gave them an honest count. All Jimmy had to do was get ahold of eight trucks, hire daily help, and have each truck make 8-10 trips a day. The money would just roll in – fifty to sixty bucks a day - and Jimmy didn't even have to get his hands dirty.

Jimmy's father was already a proud owner of two trucks, so Jimmy figured he'd have to lease out six more trucks to get the scam rolling.

When he approached his father with the scheme, the elder Fratianno told Jimmy, "No, I don't want to get into any trouble."

"What trouble?" Jimmy said. "My pal Haffey is tight with the governor of Ohio. We can't lose on this deal."

Jimmy father shook his head,

"I spent my life being honest," he said. "I'm not going to do anything crooked now."

"Ah, the heck with you," Jimmy said. "I can't make any money with you. I'll do this deal myself."

So Jimmy leased out eight trucks and paid the bribe to Haffey, in advance. Haffey worked his magic with the numbers, and in six months, Jimmy was rolling in dough.

Not bad for a man not yet twenty one years of age.

In 1934, Jimmy was already raking in the cash from his gambling business and from the landfill scam. He decided to initiate a third venture – the limousine business. Jimmy had already rubbed elbows with several members of Cleveland's underworld, which was known as "The Combination."

On the Italian side, there was the boss, Big Al Polizzi, Johnny DeMarco, and the three Angersola brothers, Johnny, Freddy and George. Heading Cleveland's Jewish crew was Moe Dalitz, "Lou Rhody" Rothkopf , and Morris Kleinman. All had gambling joints dotted throughout Cleveland, and Jimmy figured he could rake in the cash if he provided limousine service to and from all the gambling places. Of course, Jimmy needed permission for all the top guys to do this, and he had to kick back a percentage of his gross, because that's the way business is done in the underworld.

From his connection with members of "The Combination," Jimmy was introduced to the world of unions, where a guy with a lot of nerve and no conscience could do very well for himself. Jimmy had both qualifications, in spades.

Jimmy's rabbi in the union business was Bill McSweeney, who was the go-to guy when union bosses needed to put their men in line; or when wiser heads decided one particular type of business had no union and certainly needed one if they were to operate unimpeded. The 5-foot 9-inch Fratianno, met the 6-foot-3 inch McSweeney on the golf course, and the big Irishman told Jimmy he heard he had guts.

"Damn right, I have guts," Jimmy told him. "So long as the pay is square, I'm up for anything."

"Well, I'm organizing a parking lot union," McSweeney said. "And I need tough guys to convince certain parking lot owners they need to join the union."

Jimmy signed on the dotted line, and soon Jimmy was making $15 a day for himself, and an extra $10 a day for every man he signed up from The Hill to join his wrecking crew.

When McSweeney told Jimmy of a particular parking lot that needed to be brought into the fold, Jimmy, and nine guys he had recruited from the street, paraded into the parking lot. And then the fun began.

Jimmy's boys would slash tires and break windshields, while Jimmy traipsed between the cars and splashed hydrochloric acid all over the shiny bodies of Fords, Duesenbergs, Buicks and Cadillacs alike. If a head needed to be busted, a lead pipe was the weapon of choice.

Jimmy also brought his crew to crack heads on picket lines that were impeding the progress of certain favored businesses. Knitting mill workers and transportation drivers caused most of the nuisance, but after Jimmy and his boys got through with them, it was no more picket lines and the businesses went back to operating in the same manner that they did before.

In November of 1935, Jimmy got the break he had been waiting for. He was invited by the top bosses of the Combination to travel down to Miami, Florida to help them with their gambling operations, both legit and not-so-legit. Jimmy was so overjoyed at the opportunity, he bought himself a new Oldsmobile to drive to the sunny state. And as soon as he hit the Miami streets, he invested in a new warm-weather wardrobe which marked him as a mover and shaker, and not some crumbum out to hustle a few bucks.

While the Combination's big shots devoted most of their time to their new and legitimate "Plantation" gambling den, Jimmy job was to take illegal action at the racetracks, especially at Hialeah. His old gambling partner, Johnny Martin, like he did years before on The Hill, schooled Jimmy on how to operate, make money, and not get into trouble with the law.

"You see, the whole trick is not to let the guy who bets with you know you're not booking the bet yourself, but instead are laying it off on the track windows," Martin told Jimmy. "The only reason they're betting with you is that they don't want the odds to go down on the horses they're betting. So, if he knows what you're doing, he don't need you. That means you have to hire yourself a runner or two to place the bets for you.

"The second thing is, don't ever refuse a bet. You have the percentages working in your favor; just like the track does. In fact, you are the track, as far as it goes. Pay whatever the track pays, not a penny less. That way you're sure to get repeat business.

"The one thing you have to be careful with is not to take bets on hot horses. Make sure the guy is betting straight from the Racing Form and not from a hot tip someone gave him. Guys like me know which races are fixed; which horses are juiced and which ones are doped. Keep your ears to the ground. If you take bets on hot horses, you'll get killed. As for the cops, we've got them under control; and the race track guys too. Those two things aside, this is the easiest and safest way in the world to make money in the gambling business."

It was Johnny Demarco who first introduced Jimmy to the famous New York City mob boss, Lucky Luciano. This was during the time New York City Special Prosecutor, Thomas E. Dewey, was making life miserable for Lucky up north. As a result, Lucky had absconded to Miami to take the sun for a couple of months, and at the same time, and to get away from the heat.

Lucky knew the score with the Combination hooking up Jimmy to take bets at the track, and he knew Jimmy was laying off the bets at the track window. But mobsters have an unwritten code that says "let your fellow hoods make money when they can." Lucky knew, in the long run, horse betters are invariably losers, so why let the race track rake in all the cash?

Lucky had ventured to Miami with three of his pals. And they bet almost every race every day; $100 to win and $100 to place. In the span of 55 days, Jimmy earned, from Luciano's crew alone, $24,000. Johnny Martin was right. It was the easiest money Jimmy had ever made in the gambling business.

However, the following summer, a greater opportunity beckoned up north, and for Jimmy, Miami was too hot in the summer anyway.

In the summers of 1936 and 1937, the Great Lakes Exposition Fair was held in Cleveland (The site is now used for the Rock and Roll Hall of Fame). In 1935, the Fair had been held in Chicago, but it moved to Cleveland to commemorate the centennial of Cleveland being incorporated as a city. In 1936, the Fair attracted 4 million visitors. And it 1937, its last year in Cleveland, it attracted 7 million people.

The entrance to the Fair was at the north end of East 9th Street, and it went as far as East 22nd Street. Its northern boundary was Lake Erie, and it traveled south to Public Hall. All in all, the Fair covered an astounding 135 acres.

The Fair contained a floating stage where the Bob Crosby Orchestra (Bing's younger brother – there were seven Crosby brother in all) was the house band. Billy Rose's Aquacade was the main attraction, and its stars were Olympic swimming five-time gold medal winner, Johnny Weissmuller (Tarzan in the movies) and the 1932 Olympic swimming 300-yard medley gold medal winner, Eleanor Holm (Holm made the 1936 Olympic Team, but was suspended from the American team for getting drunk on a party ship during the Olympics). Holm latter married her boss, Billy Rose.

Gangsters like Jimmy knew where there are loads of people, there's plenty of cash. And where there's plenty of cash, there's guys like Jimmy to suck the green stuff out of the flush gamblers invariably included in the multitudinous crowd.

In May of 1936, Jimmy moved his gambling operation to the Great Lakes Exposition Fair, and he ran it from the midget's tent for the two full seasons. Midgets may be small in stature, but they're giants when it comes to gambling. And this fact was not lost on Jimmy Fratianno. Jimmy also made mucho dinero from, the contingent of clowns, the circus strongman and his girlfriend - the bearded lady. Outsiders were allowed in the tent to gamble, but only if they were vouched for by someone connected to the Fair.

While his gambling enterprise took up most of his daytime hours, Jimmy spent his evenings cruising Cleveland's top nightclubs, where me met future Cleveland mob boss Jack "Blackie" Licavoli and Pittsburg's mob titan Johnny LaRock (LaRocca). Jimmy also hooked up with Frank Valenti, who would later take over the town of Rochester, New York, for the mob.

But the most important person Jimmy met that summer was his future wife, Jewel Switzer. Jewel was only 18-years-old, blue-eyed, blond, buxom, and beautiful, and she was the hat check girl at the gambling joint called "The French Casino." Jimmy checked his hat, took the receipt, and next thing he knew, on August, 1, 1936, Jimmy and Jewel were standing at the altar of a non-denominational church. They said their "I do's," and two months later Jewel was pregnant. Their daughter, Joanne, was born on June, 24, 1937.

With three mouths to feed, Jimmy had to get cranking as to how make a better living. He decided, instead of running the gambling games, it was quicker and easier to rob them instead. He enlisted Tony Dope, and they knocked off two gambling joints in a row. At their first job, the two old pals from "The Hill" put on ski masks, and with each carrying a .38 caliber revolver, they busted into a private poker game in some sucker's apartment; a sucker with no real connections to the Cleveland mob.

"Okay, everybody empty out all your pockets, and put your money and jewelry on the table," Jimmy bellowed.

The six poker players, plus two workers did as they were told. Tony Dope scooped all the cash and the jewelry into a pillow case, one of several he had brought to the scene.

"Now take off all your clothes including your underwear, drop them on the floor, and then stand against the wall," Jimmy said.

There were a few grumbles from the rubes who had just been robbed, but after Jimmy pistol whipped one of the dealers, the rest fell in line – nude and face-first against the wall. Tony Dope skittered around the room, shoving the dropped clothes into several laundry bags he had brought just for the occasion. Then Tony Dope pulled the telephone wire out of the wall.

"Okay, we're leaving," Jimmy said. "And nobody gets hurt as long as long as no one follows us."

"How the fuck are we going to follow you?" one nudester bellowed out. "We ain't got no clothes!"

Smiling broadly at their genius, the two crooks exited the premises, carrying the cash and the discarded clothes in the laundry bag. When they got back to Tony Dope's place, they discovered they were $5,800 hundred dollars richer, plus whatever they could get from a fence for the jewelry. The going rate was usually 25% of the market value, and that suited Jimmy and Tony Dope just fine.

Of course, Jimmy and Tony Dope had to kick up a percentage of their take to men like "Blackie" Licavoli and Tony LaRock. And after doing so, Blackie and LaRock turned on Jimmy and Tony Dope to another big score.

This one was a high-class gambling joint run by two Jewish gentlemen out of a nightclub which had shaky connections to Moe Dalitz. Instead of just six poker players, there were about two hundred gamblers on the premises, including scores of gals, who were dressed to the nines, and of course, wearing expensive jewelry.

Jimmy and Tony Dope went in fast with shotguns, and instead of crude ski masks, they had silk stockings pulled over their faces. Jimmy threw a shotgun blast into the ceiling to get everyone's attention, knowing two detectives on the take were keeping guard outside to make sure the robbery wasn't interrupted by the law, or anyone else, for that matter.

Jimmy ordered everyone against the wall, even the gals, and he and Tony Dope fleeced the crew for over $70,000 in cash, plus the jewelry. Jimmy, ever the gentleman, and because of the presence of ladies, let everyone keep on their clothes. The two thieves exited the premises, and it was the two detectives standing guard outside who drove the getaway car, an unmarked police sedan.

Again, Jimmy and Tony Dope kicked up some nice cash to Licavoli and LaRock, and an extra five grand for Moe Dalitz, who had been in on the deal from the get-go.

Jimmy's next job, his last one for a while, involved a big-mouthed layoff bookmaker named Joe Deutsch. Blackie Licavoli sent Jimmy to straighten out Deutsch, who had missed a few of his kick-back payments. Instead of being contrite and making excuses, Deutsch, who never saw or heard of Jimmy, was not impress by Jimmy height, or his 150-pound frame.

"Fuck you, punk, I ain't paying until I'm good and ready," Deutsch told Jimmy. "Now go fuck yourself and take a walk before you get hurt."

Jimmy didn't know whether to shit or go blind. Nobody had ever talked to Jimmy like that before. But now was not the time to get stupid.

"Okay, you're clear for a while," Jimmy said. "But I'll be back."

Jimmy huddled with Tony Dope and Bill McSweeney, and with the blessing of Blackie Licavoli, they decided to give Deutsch a nasty beating, but not before robbing him of his night's take, which Jimmy figured to be about $10,000.

It was about 9:30 pm on a Saturday night when Jimmy, driving his own Buick with stolen plates, followed Deutsch through the streets of Cleveland after Deutsch had made his last pickup of the night. Sitting next to Jimmy was Tony Dope, strapped with a .38 caliber revolver. Bill McSweeney sat in the back seat fingering a .38 he had borrowed from a friend.

Deutsch stopped at a red light on the corner of Ninth Street and Superior. Before Deutsch knew what was happening, Jimmy and Tony Dope stormed his car; Jimmy on the drivers' side and Tony Dope on the passenger side. Both held hot guns in their hands, as a crowd of about 100 people milling on the streets on prime time Saturday night looked on in horror.

Jimmy stuck his gun into the side of Deutsch's head.

"Don't do anything stupid, and you won't get hurt," Jimmy said.

Deutsch, figuring this was his last Saturday night out, would have none of that.

Deutsch screamed at the top of his lungs, "Help, police!"

Jimmy yelled at Tony Dope. "Hit him in the fucking head with the gun!"

Tony Dope did as he was told, and soon Deutsch's blood was all over Jimmy's gray gabardine suit. Jimmy pulled the unconscious Deutsch from behind the wheel, and shoved him in the back seat. Then Jimmy sped off, with McSweeney following in Jimmy's Buick.

Jimmy pulled over on a quiet side street, and Tony Dope cleaned out Deutsch's pockets.

There was only $1,600, hardly the type of payout Jimmy expected after ruining his $100 suit.

They left Deutsch in the back seat of his car, and after McSweeney dumped the phony plates down a sewer and Tony Dope ditched his gun down the same sewer, they jumped into Jimmy's car, with McSweeney driving and Jimmy sitting in the back seat. They planned to head to McSweeney's digs to divvy up the cash and to clean up a bit.

"Hey, Bill, get rid of your rod too," Jimmy told McSweeney.

"Nah, I can't," McSweeney said. "I borrowed it from a pal, and since I didn't fire it, what difference does it make anyway?"

Jimmy mulled that over for a bit, and before he could come up with an answer, a police car with the siren blaring motioned for the Buick to pull over to the curb.

The cop jumped out of his car, and waving his flashlight, he saw Jimmy in the back seat covered in blood.

"What happened to you, bub?" the cop said.

"Nah, nothing," Jimmy said. "I got into a little fight over at a pool room.

The cop traded his flashlight for his police-issued revolver.

"Everybody out of the car," the cop said. "Something's fishy here."

Of course, the cop found McSweeney's gun, but even worse, another police car found Deutsch unconscious in the back seat of his car, with his pockets turned inside out. Deutsch was no rat, and he refused to say what had happened.

But after the police lab matched the blood on Jimmy's suit to Deutsch's blood, it was all over but the sentencing.

All three men were found guilty of armed robbery and were hit with ten-to-twenty five year prison sentences. Jimmy next stop was "college"; not Ohio State University in Columbus, but Ohio State Penitentiary in Youngstown instead.

Jimmy was only 23 years old at the time, but he had spent numerous hours with ex-cons on the streets talking about how to do good, productive time in prison. To most crooks, doing time is part of the life, so you needed a system in place; a system that blocks out the outside world and creates a safe cocoon to exist within, no matter what the circumstances are. So, even though this was Jimmy's first stint behind bars, he knew what to do and how to do it.

But most importantly, he learned what not to do.

Jimmy knew the trick to doing good time is forgetting the outside world even existed. Cons who obsess about their families and their friends, or a great meal, or the pleasure derived from banging a good-looking gal, were destined to become miserable in prison. Some depressed cons even ended their lives in despair.

On hardened crook once told Jimmy, "In the can, throw out the calendar and don't count the days. Sleep as much as you can and if your dick gets stiff, whack it right away. Stay away from the fags in prison. There's nothing they can do for you that you can't do for yourself. Besides, these homos are weight lifters, and as strong as any motherfucker in the can. You don't want to mess with them, so stay the fuck away. And for Christ sake, don't worry about the bedbugs, the roaches, and the rats. Prison is infested with them, so get the fuck used to them."

Jimmy also knew in prison, if you take shit from anyone, you'll get a double dose every day. Following the script exactly as the ex-cons had laid it out for him, on his first day on the chow line, Jimmy sized up the biggest guy on the line in front of him. He was a Greek fellow who was behind bars for beating up his wife so bad she needed plastic surgery just to look like a woman again. Because he had checked it out with guys in the can he knew from the streets, Jimmy knew this big gorilla wasn't connected to anybody big on the outside. And besides, a man who beats up a broad gets no sympathy behind bars.

Jimmy knew the trick was to catch him by surprise, hit him your best shot and hope to God he goes down, so that you can finish the job. Jimmy knew he needed an edge, so in right fist he held a small piece of lead that would add power to his punch. It was given to him by an old pal, Thomas "Yonnie" Licavoli, Blackie's cousin, who greeted Jimmy as soon as the prison doors closed behind him

(Yonnie Licavoli was serving life for the murder of four competing bootleggers in Toledo, Ohio).

Jimmy scanned the mess hall around him, and he saw that the screws (prison guards) were paying attention elsewhere. He pushed his way past several men who were on the chow line in front of him, and he stopped behind his intended victim. The gaff was to strike first, and then yell loud enough to wake up the dead, or the screws, who were mostly sleeping on their feet.

Jimmy hauled back and nailed the big Greek right above the right ear, while yelling, "Give me dirty looks, will ya! How's this feel?"

The big Greek stood nailed to the floor, but the right side of his head was covered in blood. As the Greek moved his right hand to his head to feel for blood, Jimmy, again aided by the small piece of lead, hit him right in the middle of his teeth. Bloody white incisors flew up into the air, and Jimmy kept on firing punches until the Greek was a large puddle of mush lying in the fetal position on the floor. Jimmy landed a few kicks, but then, two prison guards tackled him, and then they used their billy clubs to settle Jimmy down.

While the guards' attention was elsewhere, Yonnie Licavoli secreted the small piece of lead out of Jimmy's right hand, so that Jimmy wouldn't get charged with assault with a deadly weapon, which could double his prison time.

Maybe the guards saw this, and maybe they didn't. But mostly they didn't care. Prison fights are as common as the cockroaches on the walls. And in truth, it's the prisoners who run the prisons; the guards are mostly there for show and to safely work toward their pensions.

Jimmy's insubordination earned him a month in the hole. But when he was released back into the general prison population, he was a hero; a man not to be messed with and a man with special privileges anointed on him by his fellow prisoners. As for the Greek, he was transferred to either another part of the Ohio Penitentiary, or another prison altogether. Jimmy didn't know, and he didn't care. He had made his bones in prison, and he had earned new friends for beating up a bigger man who had abused a woman. Jimmy knew, prison time was hard, but it's much easier when you have friends you can depend upon.

With Jimmy back in gen-pop, Yonnie Licavoli, who was the big man on prison campus, immediately got Jimmy a cushy job in the kitchen. Yonnie also got Jimmy transferred from the cell block to a dormitory, where Yonnie himself resided.

In the spring of 1940, Jimmy got hit below the belt, but he shook off the insult like it never happened. In a letter from his father, Jimmy discovered that Jewel had gotten a quickie divorce, and was now living with Jimmy's daughter in Los Angeles with her parents.

"She still loves you," his father wrote. "But her parents made her do it!"

Jimmy chucked when he read his father's letter. He had learned his prison lesson well: "Forget about family and friends. " Even a losing a wife and child meant nothing to a man who had forgotten they existed in the first place.

Jimmy did a little more than three years at the Ohio State Penitentiary in relative comfort, but then Yonnie Licavoli offered Jimmy a better deal.

It seemed that Licavoli had a contact in the prison system who, for an under-the-table payment of $1,500, could get Jimmy transferred to the London Prison Farm, in London, Ohio. And the even better news was that Yonnie's cousin, "Blackie," would front Jimmy the money, which Jimmy could pay back, with no vig, and he got released from the can.

"When you're back on the streets and earning, the vig starts," Yonnie said. "But not until then."

Jimmy took the deal and was delighted by his transfer to the London Prison Farm, because the facility was just that – a 3000 acre farm – where inmates, housed in medium security dormitories, raised crops, milked cows, or worked in the meat processing center.

Jimmy barely worked three hours a day at the prison farm, as a "fire chief," whose main job was to see to it that there weren't any fires to extinguish. Jimmy spent most of his time playing softball to the delight of Warden William Amrine, who had his farm team, called "Amrine's Angels," play other prison softball teams all across the state.

Being a star player on the softball team (Jimmy led the league in batting average three years in a row) afforded Jimmy the privilege of living in the "honor dorm," which unlike the other dormitories at London Prison Farm, had special comfort mattresses on all the bunk beds, which were set further apart than at the other dorms on campus.

There were cells at the London Prison Farms, but they were "by request" only. There was a supposed waiting list for these cells, but in his five years at the prison farm, Jimmy never heard of anyone who actually saw this waiting list.

Jimmy's prison time was up in February 1945, but before he left, he schemed his way into paying a visit to Yonnie Licavoli back at the Ohio State Pen. Jimmy told Yonnie he was getting back with his wife, Jewel, but since her parents lived in Los Angeles, he was relocating out West.

"Jimmy, when you get to Los Angeles, I want you to hook up with Johnny Roselli," Yonnie said. "He's a good fellow from Chicago, but he's moving out West. He's in jail now, but he's coming out soon. I'll put in a good word for you. Roselli's a standup guy."

After Jimmy, now 31-years old and toughened from his time in the can, was released from prison he went back to Cleveland because he needed to earn some money before he could make the trek out to La La Land. Jimmy hooked up with old friend, Frank Valenti, and they participated in a number of stickups, again of gambling parlors.

Still, Jimmy needed a legitimate job to please his parole office. So Babe Triscaro, the business agent for the local Teamsters and in tight with Cleveland's Italian Mob (which law enforcement now called the Mayfield Road Mob), got Jimmy a no-show job at the canteens at three separate factories controlled by the union.

Managing the canteen, in which Jimmy supervised the purchase and sale of traditional household items in addition to health and personal care products, gave Jimmy the chance to get his hooks in the black market made possible by World War II. Through his contacts in the mob, Jimmy sold, from the Teamsters' canteen, things that were being rationed by the government for the American public. Nylon hose for woman was almost impossible to get legitimately, and cigarettes, liquor and particularly gas and tires for cars, were strictly rationed and could only be bought with government issued rationing stamps. Jimmy made a nice buck buying all these items, including the rationing stamp, from his mob connections, and then selling them to union members for two and sometimes three times what he had paid for them.

When black market items became scarce, Jimmy would, on tips from crooked Teamsters officials, find out which Teamsters trucks were carrying the precious goodies. Then Jimmy, with the tacit approvals of crooked union truck drivers, would hijack the trucks himself.

By 1946, the war on two fronts was over, and Jimmy, his pockets bulging with cash from a rip-roaring year of armed robberies and stealing anything that wasn't nailed down, decided it was time to get back with Jewel. This necessitated Jimmy driving his 1946 Buick to Los Angeles, with the trunk of his car loaded down with more than ninety grand in cash. As soon as Jimmy arrived in the Golden State, Jimmy and Jewel, against her parent's wishes, got married again. Jimmy, Jewel and daughter, Joanne, again became one big happy family.

Using his mob connections from Cleveland, Jimmy, with the approval and supervision of West Coast mob boss Jack Dragna, got involved in the book making business in Santa Monica. Soon, Jimmy was one of the West Coast bad boys, rubbing elbow with the likes Salvatore "Dago Louie" Piscopo, and stone killer, Frank "Bomp" Bompensiero, who would play a huge part in Jimmy's rise and fall in future years.

In September of 1947, Jimmy was invited to Dago Louie's Beverly Hills mansion to meet Johnny Roselli, who had recently been released from prison. Roselli had been arrested and convicted for extorting money from Hollywood big shots, including producers, directors, and A-list actors and actresses. Roselli had been sentenced to 10 years in prison, but then his mob pals got their hooks into the right judge, Roselli was sprung from Leavenworth Prison on August 13, 1947. He hooked up with Dragna with whom he had worked with in the past, and Roselli hit the ground running. Jimmy had heard only good things about Roselli (real name Filippo Sacco), who had performed his first hit when he was only 16years-old.

On July 4 1905, Roselli was born in Esperia, Italy, near Rome. Soon after his birth, Roselli's father, Vincenzo Sacco, made the trip by without his family on a freighter to the United States, called by the Italians - the Mountain of Gold. Six years later, Roselli and his mother took the same trip, and they hooked up with Roselli's father in Somerville, Massachusetts, just two miles north of Boston.

Roselli eschewed school and hooked up with the local racketeers. His specialty was hijacking bootlegged liquor trucks owned by competing bootleggers. In 1921, during one of Roselli's raids, he shot to death to close relative of a local Mafioso. Fearing for his life, Roselli, escaped to Chicago, where he changed he named from Sacco to Roselli, in honor of the famed Italian sculptor Cosimo Roselli.

In Chicago, Roselli hooked up with the 23-year-old Al Capone, who had recently arrived in Chicago from his hometown of Brooklyn, New York, at the request of his New York pal and fellow Five Points Gang member, Johnny Torrio. Capone and Torrio took care (murdered) Chicago boss, Big Jim Colosimo, and they assembled a group of mostly Italian gangsters which they called "The Outfit." Roselli became a huge part of the Capone/Torrio regime, and it was Big Al himself who gave Roselli the moniker of "Handsome Johnny."

By 1924, when Roselli was only 19, he was arrested for bootlegging. It was his first arrest, and after doing four months in prison, Torrio sent "Handsome Johnny" out to the virgin lands of Los Angeles, where "The ChicagoOutfit" had a lucrative racing wire business. It was also the beginning of the time when Midwest and

East Coast mobsters realized they could make a goldmine by infiltrating Hollywood's movie-related businesses. Capone figured a good-looking guy like Roselli was a natural to rub elbows with the biggest Hollywood silent stars, thereby gaining their confidence until the shrewd Roselli could figure a way to turn his Tinseltown connections into a cash cow for "The Outfit."

It was through an introduction by silent heartthrob Rudolph Valentino that Roselli met movie producer, Bryan Foy, a former vaudevillian (The Seven Little Foys) and fellow Chicagoan, who while working for Warner Brother, cranked out an average of 26 two-reel "B" movies a year. This earned earning Foy the nickname "Keeper of the B's." Whether though intimidation, or because of their Chicago connections, Foy anointed Roselli as one of his fellow producers. The former is more likely.

After forming his own production Company, "Eagle Lion Studios," Foy gave Roselli free reign in producing several of the company's gangster movies. This trend continued from the Silent Movie era into the time of the Talkies, after which silent movies became obsolete. One of the movies Roselli helped produce was the 1938 film "Crime School," which starred the Dead End Kid and Hollywood-typecast gangster, a young Humphrey Bogart. All through the late 1920's and 1930's, Roselli ingratiated himself into the inner workings of Hollywood, not because he loved the medium, but because he saw tremendous profits in infiltrating the International Alliance of Theatrical Stage Employees Union.

By the late 1930s, Al Capone was in jail and Johnny Torrio was retired. So, Roselli supposedly took his marching orders from Capone's successor, Frank Nitti. However, Nitti was considered a weak leader (he committed suicide in 1943), and the real powers in "The Outfit" were Paul "The Waiter" Ricca and the Welshman Murray "The Camel" Humphreys, the chief political fixer and labor racketeer in Chicago.

It was Humphreys who enticed Roselli to get in tight with the Hollywood unions, and to fleece them for every penny Roselli could get for "The Outfit." This was not hard to do, since Hollywood is a town of "make believe," and Roselli's world was based on one cold hard fact: "If you apply enough pressure, the bozos in Hollywood would give you anything you want."

Roselli knew the Hollywood crowd was afraid and too unsophisticated in the ways of the underworld to challenge Roselli, or his authority. In 1939, the 33-year-old Roselli married the beautiful 22-year-old Hollywood actress June Lang. But that didn't stop Roselli from impregnating another actress Hollywood, Helen Greco, in 1941.

In 1942, Roselli's extortion of the Hollywood unions came to an abrupt end. And it was a Jewish gangster from Chicago, who was sent to Hollywood by Frank Nitti who started the house of cards to tumble.

In 1935, after Roselli had already his hooks in deep in Hollywood, Willie Bioff was sent out West to assist Roselli in his rackets. While Roselli was the good-looking and sweet-talking operator, Bioff was a short, squat, and unattractive version of the 1930s Hollywood gangster. While Roselli had class, Bioff was a crude thug who personally made the collections from the unions (and not too nicely), and he filtered the cash back to Chicago.

One Hollywood insider said of Bioff, "Forget his fancy suits and solid gold business cards. Bioff's still an ugly mug with a high profile."

This high profile put Bioff on law enforcement's radar and also caught the attention of syndicated columnist Westbrook Pelger, who was causing havoc in Chicago for his *Chicago Tribune's* exposes on the mob's influence in the labor unions. Pelger set his sights on Bioff, and it was all downhill for Bioff after that (Pelger won a 1941 Pulitzer Prize for his articles on corrupt unions).

In 1943, the inevitable happened. Bioff was arrested on an assortment of crimes, including "income tax evasion" - the same crime that had destroyed Al Capone. Rather than do time, Bioff laid out for the feds the entire scheme that he and Roselli had perpetrated in Hollywood (Nitti committed suicide the day after Bioff became a canary). Bioff told the feds Roselli was his boss in L.A., but he also implicated Nitti, Ricca, and Murray Humphreys, who somehow avoided prosecution.

In late 1942, as soon as Roselli got wind that Bioff was ready to fold, Roselli got sudden pangs of patriotism. He joined the United States Army, where he became a lowly buck private working in the mess hall. This ploy worked for a while, but when the feds found Roselli was actually one of their own employees, on March 19,

1943, Roselli was arrested while doing KP duty at the Tinker Air Force base just southeast of Oklahoma City. Roselli was then dispatched to Chicago face the federal charges of "racketeering." Also indicted with Roselli were Chicago mobsters, Paul Ricca, Charles Gioe, Phil D'Andrea, Louis Campagna, Frank Maritote, and Ralph Pierce, who was dropped from the case after the trial started.

The trial, which began on October, 5, 1943, lasted until December 22 of the same year. Willie Bioff's testimony was devastating to the defense, and all six men were found guilty of a conspiracy to extort more than $1 million from the motion picture industry. Each man received a prison sentence of 10 years and a $10,000 fine.

But with Murray "The Camel" Humphreys pulling the necessary strings, all six men were released on parole in mid-1947. It was rumored that Humphreys was so politically connected, he arranged for the parole of his crew men directly though Tom C. Clark, the Attorney General under President Harry S. Truman, a Midwestern boy from Missouri.

As for Bioff, Humphreys pulled some different stings to find out where Bioff had been relocated by the government after he did a measly 16 months in the can. It turned out that Bioff was nice and snuggy in Arizona, and in tight with Arizona Senator Barry Goldwater. Bioff (his new name was "William Nelson") even went into business with Goldwater's nephew, Bobby Goldwater.

His confidence soaring and his connections to famous politicians at its peak, Bioff took a trip to Las Vega, where he got, though his political connections, a job working for the Riviera Hotel for Gus Greenbaum, an old pal from Chicago. Bioff, obviously delusional, stark raving mad, or both, never figured Greenbaum would turn Bioff in to the "Chicago Outfit." Actually, Greenbaum did remain silent about Bioff for several years, and in fact, both men were skimming from the skim Greenbaum was supposed to send back to his bosses in Chicago. When Chicago found out about his chicanery, Greenbaum threw them Bioff as a peace offering. The Outfit took the gift, and told Greenbaum to get lost. Greenbaum wound up in Phoenix, Arizona; gone but not forgotten.

On November 4, 1955, Bioff exited his tony home in the suburbs of Las Vegas and jumped into his spiffy new Ford F250 pick-up truck. He turned the ignition, and soon parts of the truck and pieces of Bioff's body had been propelled throughout the neighborhood. A police investigation uncovered that several sticks of dynamite had been wired to the truck's starter.

As for Greenbaum, "The Outfit" let him live a little more than three years longer than Bioff. On December 3, 1958, Greenbaum and his wife, Bess, were found dead in their Phoenix homes. Both their throats had been cut with a butcher knife.

When Jimmy "The Weasel" Fratianno finally met Johnny Roselli at Dago Louie's house, what impressed Jimmy most was Roselli's wardrobe.

"All us West Coast guys wore the flashiest clothes, but Roselli was different," Jimmy said. "Johnny wore conservative business suits, and if you didn't know better, you'd think he was a banker, or maybe even an accountant."

After a scrumptious dinner of fine Italian food, Jimmy cornered Roselli out by Dago Louie's pool. Jimmy relayed to Roselli the message Yonnie Licavoli had given him before Jimmy was released from prison.

"Yonnie told me to look you up when you got out of prison," Jimmy said. "He said you could straighten me out with the right people."

Roselli took Jimmy by the arm, and he led Jimmy back into the house and into a private room. They sat on two leather arm chairs, facing each other. As he spoke, Jimmy could smell the wine on Roselli's breath.

"Do you understand what Yonnie meant when he said to 'straighten you out'?" Roselli said.

"Sure I do, Johnny," Jimmy said. "I've been wanting this since I was a kid. I knew the Italians on the Hill had something special thing going for them, but it's so hard to get installed into their group."

Roselli smiled, and said, "That's right, and that's the way it should be. If the wrong guy gets made, you've got to clip him right away. This thing of ours is no joke. They don't give you a pink slip when they want to get rid of you."

"Well, what do you think, Johnny," Jimmy said. "Do I have a chance here, or not?"

"Look, I just met you, but Yonnie doesn't give recommendations too easy," Roselli said. "Let me ask around about you. We need new blood here on the West Coast. But I need to know for sure that you're a capable guy."

Roselli did his due diligence on Jimmy, and Jimmy got rave reviews, not only from Yonnie Licavoli, but from Dago Louie, and also from Jack Dragna, the supposed head of the West Coast mob. But those in the know understood that Dragna was mostly a figurehead, and Roselli was the conduit who relayed the instructions from the big boys in the Midwest. When Roselli checked with Cleveland, Jimmy got high marks too, and the Cleveland bosses gave Roselli the okay to make Jimmy in Los Angeles. After all, Roselli didn't want to step on the wrong toes and get himself in the middle of something he should have kept his nose away from.

In late October 1947, Jimmy was summoned to a small winery on South Figueroa Street in Los Angeles. He was told to wear his best suit, which was an indication he might finally be inducted into the West Coast branch of Chicago's Outfit. Either that, or Jimmy was being sent there to get whacked. In this business, you never knew when the lights will go out.

It was just after dark, when Jimmy knocked on the winery front door, and it was Johnny Roselli himself who opened the door and greeted him. As Jimmy entered the winery, he spotted a huge crowd of other Italians milling about in the winery's oversized conference room; some Jimmy knew and others were total strangers.

"Come in, Jimmy," Roselli said. "We've been waiting for you."

Jimmy hesitated for a second, and Roselli smiled.

"Don't worry, you're not here to get clipped," Roselli said. "Come inside, and after you've taken the oath, I want you circle the room, kiss everybody on the cheek and introduce yourself to men you don't know."

Jimmy strode into the conference room, and the first thing he noticed was the strong smell of wine. Then he spotted three men who he had worked closely with for the past three years sitting at the head of the table. They were Jack Dragna, ostensibly the West Coast boss of "The Outfit," his brother Tom Dragna, and Jack Dragna's underboss, Momo Adamo.

When he spotted Jimmy, Jack Dragna stood and announced to the crowd, "I want everyone to stand up, form a circle and hold hands."

Jimmy was told to stand at a place at the table with five other men, at a spot where a gun and a dagger were crisscrossed in front of them. This is when Jimmy realized, that beside himself, five more men were set to be inducted that night, including Tom Dragna's son, Louie Dragna.

Jack Dragna then addressed the crowd in a mixture of the Sicilian dialect and Italian, which Jimmy had trouble understanding. Jimmy's family was from Naples, and the Sicilians speak in a bastardized version of Italian that few non-Sicilians Italians can understand. At best, Jimmy understood only a few words and phrases.

With Johnny Roselli helping with the translation, Jimmy understood Jack Dragna to say, "This secret society of ours welcomes only men of great courage and loyalty. You come in alive and you go out dead. There is no other way. The gun and the knife are the instruments by which you live and die.

"This thing of ours (La Cosa Nostra) comes first before anything else in your life. It comes before your family, country, and even before God. When you are summoned, you must come, even if your mother, your wife and children are on their deathbed. If you fail to do so, the punishment is death without a trial, or warning.

"There are three laws you must obey without question. You must never betray any of our secrets. You must never violate the wife or children of another member. And you must never become involved in narcotics. If you violate any of these laws, again the punishment is death. Do you understand?"

The five inductees nodded yes.

One by one, each of the five men were told to raise the index finger of their right hand. Johnny Roselli pricked each index finger with a small pin, causing droplets of blood to form.

Jack Dragna continued his drone.

"This drop of blood symbolizes your birth into our family. We are now one until death."

Jack Dragna strolled around the table, and he embraced the five new inductees and kissed them on both cheeks, saying to each individually, "You are now a made guy, an *amico nostra*, a *soldato* in our famiglia. Whenever you wish to introduce a member to another member he doesn't know, you say, "*Amico Nostra*. In English you say, 'This is a *friend of ours*.' But whenever you introduce a member to someone who's not a member, your say, 'This is a *friend of mine*.'"

The ceremony at its end, Jimmy made the rounds of the room, shaking hands, kissing cheeks and introducing himself to other *amico nostra*.

Jimmy knew one thing for sure; he was now a made man who had a license from the underworld to do whatever he damned well pleased. Murdering, robbing, extorting, and giving out beatings were all permissible in the secret society. As long as the victim was not a made man, or a relative of a made man. Friends, or associates of made men were a different story.

Sometimes you had to get permission to do something drastic. But if you were intent on doing something bad to someone you suspect was connected, you could always play stupid, and claim you didn't know the connection.

Jimmy knew this happened every day in "This thing of ours."

"Men of Honor" lie and cheat, and even kill for one reason only – money. Because, except for law enforcement's possible involvement after the fact, made men could always get away with just about anything; even murder, and sometimes, especially murder.

And Jimmy "The Weasel" Fratianno planed on doing whatever he could to increase his wealth and increase his prestige in the underworld. And no one, even other made men, was going to stop him.

Jimmy's biggest impediment to making a decent buck in Los Angeles, and his crew's most annoying distraction, was Jewish mobster and ex-professional boxer, the pugnacious Mickey Cohen.

Cohen was born Meyer Harris Cohen on September 4, 1913, in the Brownsville section of Brooklyn, New York, which was the future stomping grounds for Louie "Lepke" Buchalter's Murder Incorporated. After Mickey's father died when Cohen was just a toddler, Mickey's mother, a Russian-Jewish immigrant from Kiev in the Ukraine who spoke almost no English, took Mickey and his five older siblings to Boyle Heights, a mixed-nationality working class neighborhood where a young boy had to fight almost every day just to survive.

Mickey, a constant delinquent from school, was a tough little scrapper, and by the time he was 10, Mickey had already done two stints in reform school. When he turned 12, Mickey got a job working in an older brother's drug store, where they made bootleg booze in the back room. At the age of 15, Mickey figured he could make a few bucks with his fists, and it was totally legal. Well, almost. After engaging in a few "smokers" or illegal prize fights were the winners won a cheap watch, Mickey moved to Cleveland to work with professional boxing trainers.

On October 3, 1930, when he was only 16, Mickey turned pro in the lightweight division. He won his first three fights, but then he hit a downward spiral where he lost nine of his last ten fights; the last five in a row, and last three by knockout. His final boxing record was 7 wins, 11 losses and one draw. He scored only one knockout.

In October 1932, Mickey moved back to the West Coast. And to Mickey's credit, or due to the influence of his managers, Mickey's last two losses were knockouts at the hands of future world champions Chalky Wright (April 11, 1933) and Baby Arizmendi (May 14, 1933). Mickey also was knocked out in one round by world champion Tommy Paul on June 12, 1931. The fight was so action-packed for as long as it lasted (2 minutes and 20 seconds), after the fight Mickey was given the moniker "Gangster Mickey Cohen."

By the time he decided to quit getting beat up in the ring, Mickey had become fast pals with Johnny "Johnny Dio" Dioguardi, who had a stranglehold on the New York City unions, especially in the garment district. Through Johnny Dio, Cohen became acquainted with fellow Jewish mobsters, Meyer Lansky and Bugsy Siegel, and it was Siegel who took Cohen back to California to help him with his Hollywood shakedowns. Cohen was also passed around liberally by the mob to Chicago and Cleveland to do whatever "convincing" needed to be done to people who, to the mob's way of thinking, needed convincing. This is where Cohen's boxing background served him well.

In his travels, Cohen became tight with Cleveland's Jewish mob boss, Moe Dalitz, and also with several higher ups in Chicago's outfit, including Frank Milano who was the boss of the Mayfield Road Mob from the early 1920's until 1935, when Milano was forced to flee to Mexico on a tax evasion charge.

By the time Jimmy Fratianno got his button in the West Coast mob, due to the fact that Bugsy Siegel had been exterminated by his mob pals for skimming off the top of his skim at the Flamingo Hotel in Las Vegas, Mickey Cohen was the biggest bookmaker on the West Coast. The problem for Jimmy's crew, under Jack Dragna, was that Cohen had cheery-picked some of Dragna's best men and put them to work for himself, at a much higher salary than the notorious cheapskate, Dragna, was used to paying. At stake was the reported $80,000-a-week bookmaking business Cohen controlled in Los Angeles.

Jimmy fired the first salvo at Cohen when, on the 1949 Labor Day weekend, he invited mobster Frank Niccoli to his home on Holy Cross Place in the Westchester section of Los Angeles. Niccoli had been of Dragna's best men, but he had bolted ship and started working for Mickey Cohen. Dragna ordered Jimmy to convince Niccoli to come back into the fold.

When Niccoli walked through the front door of Jimmy's house, he was surprised not to see Jimmy wife, Jewel, or his daughter Joanne.

"Where's the wife and kid?" Niccoli said.

"They're in Toledo visiting friends," Jimmy said. "That why I invited you here today, so that we could talk in private without any distractions."

After inviting Niccoli to sit on the living room couch, Jimmy handed Niccoli his favorite Chivas and soda, and he opened a can of Acme beer for himself.

"What's on your mind?" Niccoli said.

Jimmy sat on the couch next to Niccoli.

"Mickey Cohen is on my mind," Jimmy said. "How thing's going with you and Mickey's crew?"

"It fuckin' sucks," Niccoli said. "All the rats are deserting a sinking ship. High Pockets took a powder back to Cleveland, and Jimmy Regace has gone back with your crew."

"How come you're staying with Mickey?" Jimmy said. "You know we'd like you back with us, don't you?"

"Yeah, Jimmy, I know, but me and Mickey go back a long ways," Niccoli said. "I absolutely love the guy. And he ain't stingy like Jack Dragna."

Jimmy stood up and hovered over Niccoli.

"You know, I'm going to lay it on the line to you," Jimmy said. "We want you back with us, and things could go bad for you real fast if you don't come back into the fold."

Now it was Niccoli who jumped to his feet.

"Well, that ain't happening," Niccoli said. "I'm with Mickey all the way, and if it comes to a war, I'm on Mickey's sides. Get it?"

Jimmy shook his head.

"Look I'm asking you to reconsider," Jimmy said. "But if you don't, then get out of town. Besides, what is it with you? Mickey's a Jew and you're Italian. You belong with us."

"I'm sorry," Niccoli said. "I'm sticking with Mickey."

Just then the doorbell rang.

"Sit down, and I'll get you another Chivas," Jimmy said.

Jimmy strode to the front door. He opened it and in walked the 6-foot two-inch, 250-pound Joseph "Joe Dip" Dippolito and Sammy Bruno. Jimmy left the front door open.

"Hey guys, it's a surprise to see you," Jimmy said. He turned to Niccoli. "So you know Joe Dip and Sammy?"

Niccoli stood, and he ambled to the door. He extended his right hand to Joe Dip.

"I'm pleased to meet you guys," Niccoli said.

As soon as Joe Dip had Niccoli's hand in a vice-like grip, Nick Licata and Carmine Carpinelli burst through the front door. Joe Dip spun Niccoli around and grabbed him in a reverse bear hug.

Nick Licata pulled out a length of strong rope, and before he wrapped it around Niccoli's neck, Jimmy said, "Give me the fuckin' rope. This is my job."

Jimmy twirled the rope twice around Niccoli's neck, and with Jimmy holding one end, and Nick Licata the other, they began choking the life out of Frank Niccoli. While Jimmy and Licata pulled in opposite directions with all their might, Joe Dip held Niccoli in place, Niccoli, his eyes bulging from his head and a surprised look on his face, took a leak right on Jimmy's new rug. Jimmy belched out a disgusted moan.

Sam Bruno, who was just casually surveying the situation, quipped, "Hey, don't complain, you're lucky," Bruno said. "Sometimes they even shit."

After Niccoli was dead, Joe Dip dropped him to the floor.

Jimmy said to Joe Dip, "You know what to do."

Joe Dip and Carmine Carpinelli went out to their car and retuned with two large mail bags. In the meantime, Jimmy and Sammy Bruno had stripped Niccoli naked. They stuffed Niccoli's corpse in one mailbag, and his clothes in the other. Sam Bruno went out front and parked Joe Dip's car in Jimmy's garage. After the garage door was shut, Joe Dip flung the bag with Niccoli's dead body over his shoulder, like he was delivering the mail, and he lugged the bag into the garage. Sam Bruno opened the trunk of his car, and Joe Dip flung the bag into the trunk, followed by the second bag containing Niccoli's clothes.

"Fuck!" Jimmy said to Sam Bruno. "I got me a hernia just looking at Joe Dip carrying that bag with the stiff."

Jimmy opened the garage door, and Joe Dip drove out of the garage.

Jimmy turned to Sam Bruno.

"I better clean up that piss on my rug," Jimmy said. "I hope it don't leave a stain."

An hour after he left Jimmy's garage, Joe Dip deposited both mail bags into the six-foot-deep hole he had previously dug in a vineyard he owned in Cucamonga. Joe Dip coved the bags with lime, and then he filled in the hole.

Niccoli's body was never found, and Mickey Cohen never knew what happened to one of his best men. Cohen never gave Jimmy or anyone else any indication of what he thought had happened to Niccoli. But Mickey Cohen, not punchy from all the blows he took in the ring, immediately stepped up his security, even paying off-duty Los Angeles policemen to surround him when he was out in public.

Jimmy decided the best way to clip Mickey Cohen was to plant bomb under his house.

One night while Cohen and his wife, Lavonne, were out night-club hopping with two paid off-duty cops at their side (Cohen always traveled with police bodyguards), Jimmy slipped over to Cohen's house for a look-see at the situation. Jimmy was delighted when he spotted an air vent in the back of the house which fed into Cohen's bedroom. Jimmy figured it was about 18 inches below Cohen's bed, which was about 15 feet from the back of the house. Jimmy rushed back to tell Jack Dragna the good news.

"It's a perfect set-up," Jimmy told Dragna. "When Cohen is away from home, all I have to do is remove the screen and toss the bomb in there about seven-eight feet. It will be right under that Jew bastard's bed. Then when I'm sure he's home and in bed, I'll use about a 25-foot fuse, so I'll have time to get the hell out of there. That fuse will burn for about 15 minutes, so I won't even be around when Cohen's house goes boom."

"What about his wife?" Dragna said. "We don't want to kill an innocent woman. All the heat in Los Angeles will come down on us in no time. We don't need that kind of aggravation."

"Don't worry about that," Jimmy said, "That's the beauty of this thing. Mickey has what they call a ranch-style house, and Lavonne has her own bedroom on the other side of the house."

The next night, around 9 p.m., Jimmy got a call from Jack Dragna.

"My guys spotted Cohen and his wife in a nightclub," Dragna said. "Shoot over to his house now and plant the bomb."

Jimmy got in touch with Jimmy Regace (he later changed his name to Dominick Brooklier) to drive the getaway car. Fifteen minutes later, Regace parked right in front of Mickey Cohen's house. Jimmy removed his shoes not to make any noise, and he scurried across Cohen's lawn and around to the back of the house. Jimmy unscrewed the screen on the air vent. With his right hand, Jimmy flung the bomb, which consisted of six sticks of dynamite connected to a long fuse, through the air vent. He had about 15 feet of fuse remaining outside the vent.

Jimmy hurried back to Regace's car, and they sped out of the neighborhood. They rushed over to Jimmy house to wait for a phone call to finish the job.

About 4 a.m., the phone rang. Jimmy picked it up, and Jack Dragna was on the other end.

"Happy Meltzer tailed Cohen, and he got home about three hours ago," Dragna said. "Go back there and light the fuse."

This time Regace dropped Jimmy off two blocks from Cohen's house. Jimmy took off his shoes again. He crept to Cohen's house and quiet as a church mouse, he slipped around back. Jimmy lit the fuse, and made sure it was sparking properly. When the fuse had advanced about a foot, Jimmy smiled.

He said in barely a whisper, "Bye, bye, you Jew bastard."

Grinning like a loon, Jimmy split the scene and rushed back to Regace's car. Jimmy jumped in the passenger seat, and Regace sped to the Riviera Country Club a few blocks away, where they waited for the sound of the explosion.

It never came.

A few days later, Cohen's next door neighbor spotted the wire coming out of the air vent. She notified Cohen, and he called the police. The cops found the undetonated bomb. Luckily for Mickey Cohen, the fuse had stopped burning about five feet from the dynamite.

From that point on, Cohen hired several off-duty cops to park in eight-hour shifts in front of his house.

But Jimmy was not deterred. Mickey Cohen had to go.

Jack Dragna's Trojan horse in Cohen's camp, Happy Meltzer, had accompanied Cohen in his club hopping almost every night for the past year. He told Jack Dragna that the two stops Cohen made nightly were the Plymouth House and Sherry's. Sherry's had the best setup to ambush Cohen, because right across the street next to the Bing Crosby Building was a flight of steps that led down to a vacant parking lot. Two gunmen could hide down the steps, just far enough so that they could see the entrance to Sherry's, but the people in front of Sherry's couldn't see them.

Late one Saturday night, Dragna called Jimmy with the good news. Cohen was in Sherry's and ready to be taken.

"Great," Jimmy said. "Who do you got to go with me?"

"Jimmy you're sitting this one out," Dragna said. "You're too old to be crouching down on your knees for two, three hours. I'm using the kid, Jimmy Regace. His looking to get his button and this might do it for him. Plus, I'm putting in this other kid, Army (Arthur DiMaria), who's a made guy from Vegas with Benny Binion."

"Okay," Jimmy said. "I'll drive getaway. Get me a car with stolen plates."

"That's already covered," Dragna said. "I got Scozzari (Simone) driving getaway. They're on their way over to Sherry's now."

"Who's Cohen's rat-bastard cop bodyguard tonight?" Jimmy asked.

"It's Harry Cooper, from the state's district attorney office," Dragna said.

"Our guys better be good shots," Jimmy said. "If Cooper gets hurt, we could have a problem."

"Fuck Cooper," Dragna said. "He deserves to get hit for protecting a piece of shit like Mickey Cohen."

Cohen had entered Sherry's, at 9039 Sunset Boulevard, at about 1 am. With Cohen was his girlfriend, the 26-year-old Dee Davis, a movie extra aspiring to be an actress, 39-year-old Special Agent Harry Cooper (who was a head-and-a-half taller than the diminutive Cohen), and Cohen's henchman, the 35-year-old Edward "Neddie" Herbert, who just three months earlier had escaped a barrage of 11 bullets in a gangland ambush. Cohen's entourage joined Hollywood columnist Florabel Muir and her husband Danny Morrison, and the group sat at a large circular table in the back of the restaurant. Muir pumped Cohen for some juicy tidbits for her column, but Mickey Cohen brushed her off

"What's there to tell ya?" Cohen told Muir. "There's a bunch of bums after me. But it's nothing I can't handle

At around 3:55 am, Sherry's manager, Barney Ruditski, a former flatfoot from New York City, told Cohen's crew it was closing time. This was right after Ruditski had made a cursory inspection of inside and outside the joint, looking for anyone who might be looking for Mickey Cohen. Cohen liked Ruditski, and one of the reason's Cohen made Sherry's his usual last stop was for the added protection an ex-cop like Ruditski provided.

As Ruditski later told the Los Angeles police, "Every night that Mickey Cohen came in, for the protection of my customers. I sort of watched the place and walked around outside and inside."

Not seeing any problems inside or outside the premises, Ruditski told the parking lot attendant next door to bring around the Cohen group's cars.

Cohen and his pals waited out front for their cars, and just as Regace and Army pointed their rifles from the steps to the sunken parking lot across the street, Police Sergeant Darryl Murray pulled up to the curb in front of Sherry's in his blue and white standard Los Angeles Ford police squad car with gold lettering. With the red globe siren blaring on the roof of the car, Murray stepped out of the car, and he shook Cohen's hand.

"Did someone just rob a bank?" Cohen asked Murray. "You're waking up the dead with that fuckin' siren."

"Nah, I'm just giving you a police escort back home," Murray said.

Cohen smiled, "That's the least you should do for the money I stake you guys."

Just then, the parking lot attendant pulled up in front of Sherry's with Cohen's Cadillac. As soon as the parking lot attendant exited the Caddy, a fuselage of shotgun bullets blasted into the crowd from the sunken steps across the street. Cohen took one slug in the shoulder, and he dropped to one knee behind his Caddy. But the bullet did not strike bone, and it was a simple flesh wound.

Herbert was not so lucky. He took one slug in the stomach, one in his spine, and one in his kidney. He died ten days later from uremic poisoning. Dee David took one slug in the stomach and one in the groin, but her injuries were non-life-threatening.

Harry Cooper was hit twice in the belly, and he was at death's door before he recovered two weeks later. The doctors said Cooper's size (six-foot four-inches and 225 pounds), and great physical condition enabled the former California highway patrolman to survive the shooting.

Crack Hollywood scribe, Florabel Muir, was hit once in the buttocks, but her typing fingers remained unharmed. After summoning a photographer to the scene, the carrot-topped Muir, blood seeping down the back of her dress, helped the police search for spent shotgun shells across the street in the sunken parking lot.

The following day, Muir, after refusing medical attention, wrote an exclusive on the shooting for the *Los Angeles Mirror*.

After Regace and Army had emptied their shotguns, Scozzari pulled up by the steps to the sunken parking lot in a stolen 1949 Oldsmobile with stolen plates and an overhead-valve V-8 engine. Regace and Army jumped into the Olds, and Scozzari burned rubber pulling away. Patrolman Murray jumped in police Ford and gave chase, but Scozzari was too quick and too savvy on the streets of Los Angeles, and he lost Murray in the tangle of the Los Angeles streets which intersected at extreme angles.

The day after the shooting, Attorney General Fred Howser, held a press conference at the podium of the auditorium of Police Headquarters. The reporters bombarded Howser with questions as to why one of his personal detectives, Cooper, had been at the scene of the shooting and in the presence of a thug like Mickey Cohen.

"I assigned agent Cooper to guard Cohen after his attorney, Sam Rummel, came to me and said Cohen was in fear of his life," Howser said. "We had special information as to the source which might attempt to assassinate Cohen."

One reporter refused to buy Howser's blather.

"Mickey Cohen is reported to be a top mob leader in Los Angeles," this scribe said. "He has been involved with criminals like Bugsy Siegel, and he even once worked for Al Capone in Chicago. Why is he being afforded protection not given to the average citizens of this city?"

Howser cleaned his throat, and he wiped the sweat from his forehead with a powder blue silk handkerchief.

"The circumstances will testify as to the authority of the information," Howser said. "But we are not allowed to divulge any other details at this time, or at any other time, for that matter."

Further investigation discovered that not only were Cooper and Patrolman Murray protecting Cohen on the night of the shooting, but earlier that night, three other Los Angeles cops also had the "Cohen watch" at various intervals.

It was later learned, that Mickey Cohen had a rabbi embedded in California politics. His name was Senator Arthur Samish, who was so egotistical he once declared he could "push through any laws or stop them cold." One of Samish's protégés was the aforementioned Howser, who, in 1946, prosecuted Bugsy Siegel for simple bookmaking, but refused to prosecute Mickey Cohen for the shooting death of rival, Max Shuman, because Cohen swore on a stack of bibles it was "self-defense."

Hours after Howser's press conference, his agents rounded up five suspects in the Cohen shooting. One was Joseph Messina, who although he was a barber by trade, was named the "chief suspect" by Howser. Another was journalist James Tarantino, who with Frank Sinatra's financial backing became the editor/publisher of the *Hollywood Nightlife*. Arrested with Tarantino was his "advertising salesman," Joe Tenner, who was once pinched for pandering, or the pimping of Los Angeles prostitutes. The other two arrestees were Kansas City mobsters, Anthony Trombino and Anthony Brancato, who were presumably pinched because they just happened to be in town.

All five men were released hours later due to the lack of evidence.

Not being able to kill Cohen, Dragna and Fratianno concentrated on going after Cohen's men instead. On October 10, 1949, Dave Ogul disappeared from the face of the earth. Two days later, his car was found at the corner of Sunset and Hollywood Drive.

Cohen now had four men still working directly under him: Happy Meltzer, who had set up Ogul for the kill, Eli Lubin, Jimmy Rist, and Lou Swartz. All four men surrendered themselves at the country jail, allegedly for protection purposes. And all four men refused Cohen's offer of bail.

For Jack Dragna, it was back to the "bomb Cohen" scenario.

Dragna made the bomb himself, and he directed Sam Bruno to deposit the bomb under Cohen's house. This time Dragna didn't care who was in the house with Cohen; they would have to be considered casualties of war.

Bruno planted the bomb without incident, and on February 6, 1950 at 4:15 a.m., Mickey Cohen was awaken from a deep sleep by his home burglar alarm. Not sure if an intruder was on the premises, Cohn grabbed his gun and inspected the insides of the entire house. He could see nothing amiss. But he did detect the slight smell of smoke somewhere in the distance. Cohen figured one of his neighbors had lit kindle wood in their fireplace, which explained the smell.

Cohen went back to bed, and as soon as he pulled the covers up to his chin, an explosion that sounded like an earthquake shook the house right down to its foundation. When the smoke cleared, Cohen opened his eyes and saw a hole as big as he was in the bedroom wall leading to the living room.

Cohen's walk-in closet took the biggest hit. Cohen's entire wardrobe was in shambles; his suits were shredded, and his shoes had exploded into unrecognizable shapes. On further examination, Cohen discovered every window in the house had exploded, as did the windows of every house in the neighborhood.

Luckily, Cohen was uninjured, as was his wife, his live-in maid, and his Pomeranian named Tuffy. It seemed when Sam Bruno put the bomb under Cohen's house, he put it directly under a huge steel floor safe that Cohen had installed so he wouldn't have to lug his money to the bank. The safe absorbed most of the explosion and directed it downward, but the bomb left a crater ten feet deep under Cohen's house. Luckily for Cohen, the safe contained no money, otherwise his cash would have been scattered in all directions to the delight of his neighbors.

Cohen's favorite cops arrived at his house just minutes after the explosion. One flatfoot told Cohen it looked like the house would have to be torn down, the foundation laid again, and the house rebuilt from scratch.

"Fuck the house," Cohen told the fuzz. "They ruined all my fuckin' suits, shirts, and shoes. My entire wardrobe is gone. I better not find those cocksuckers who did this."

Two weeks later, Sam Bruno got another shot at Cohen. Tom Dragna, with Bruno in the passenger seat, parked a stolen car across the street from a dive bar Cohen was seen entering an hour earlier. Cohen's Caddy was parked out front, and when Bruno saw Cohen leaving the bar alone, his trigger finger tightened.

For no discernable reason, just as Bruno pulled the trigger, Cohn bent down to examine a scratch on the Caddy's bumper. The shots missed Cohen, but Bruno ventilated Cohen's Caddy with six bullets.

Jack Dragna and Jimmy Fratianno were befuddled. Four times they thought Cohen was a goner, the only damaged done to Cohen was a winging shoulder, a bulleted-holed Caddy, a crater under his house, and the mass destruction of 50 suits, 75 pair of shoes and 200 shirts.

In November 1950, a few weeks after the failed Bruno shooting, the IRS did what Dragna and his boys couldn't. Because of the high profile he maintained, Cohen came under the spotlight of the Kefauver Committee's investigation into organized crime. As a result, IRS agents arrested Cohen and his wife, Lavonne, and charged them with filing false tax returns from 1946-1949. In 1951, Cohen was convicted and sentenced to four years in jail and fined $200,000, which Cohen claimed he did not possess. Cohen told the court he spent it all on attorney's fees.

Cohen's wife, Lavonne, was acquitted on all charges. But to satisfy the IRS, their newly rebuilt house was sold at auction for $47,000.

The IRS kept the proceeds of the sale.

Tony Brancato and Tony Trombino had no respect for anyone. They were armed robbers and killers, plain and simple, and they had no conscience. They didn't care who they robbed, even if was a joint owned by the Outfit in Chicago.

In the late 1940s, Norfia Brancato was a dependable worker for Mickey Cohen. Norfia was considered a gentleman, and he showed people, mobsters and civilians alike the proper respect. So when Norfia asked Cohen to hire his younger brother, Tony, who was gangstering in Kansas City, Cohen figured, "Why not? If Tony is half as good as his brother, I've got myself a good worker."

Soon after Tony Brancato started working for Cohen, he convinced Cohen to take on his pal, Tony Trombino, a small-time hood who was still in Kansas City knocking over candy stores. Cohen said okay, but by 1951, Cohen had his own problems, trying to avoid bombs and bullets and the clutches of the IRS. So he left the two Tonys unsupervised.

That was a big mistake.

In Mickey Cohen's bio, *Mickey Cohen, My Own Words* Cohen described the two Tonys situation as such.

"I figured that Tony Brancato was a street wise kid, and at first he was a good worker," Cohen said. "But then he started stepping out on his own. He was on the heavy and on the heist, but he was heisting people that were contrary to the rules of the people that he was supposed to have respected – not only me, but others. They were wild-haired young bloods, him and Tony Trombino, who thought they were just going to run roughshod over everybody. Well, I couldn't pay them much attention then. But because of my troubles, they thought they didn't have to show any respect for nobody. They began to muscle people, to bulldoze people, and they were the wrong people. These are things that are uncalled for in this part of the country."

Both Tonys had been arrested numerous times in Kansas City, but when Cohen went to jail, they doubled down on their crime output. By the middle of 1951, the two Tonys had a combined record of 46 arrests and 17 convictions. Their crimes included rape, aggravated assault, armed robbery, burglary, and narcotics violations. In addition, the police suspected them of as many as six murders.

Although he was working in California for Jack Dragna, Jimmy Fratianno, with Bugsy Siegel dead and Mickey Cohen in prison, was in charge of the Outfits' Las Vegas operations. One of his operatives was Hy Goldberg, who ran a booking operation out of Las Vegas and also one in Beverly Hills. The two Tonys had robbed Goldberg's Beverly Hills book several times. The last time exasperated Goldberg.

Looking down the barrel of two .38 caliber pistols, Goldberg told the two Tonys, "Oh no, not again. Please tell me you're kidding this time!"

Tony Trombino stuck his gun under Goldberg's nose.

"Does it look like we're kidding?" he said.

After they hit Goldberg's book in Las Vegas for $3,500 in cash, Goldberg went to the cops, and they put out a warrant for the two Tonys arrests.

But the two Tonys weren't finished.

A few weeks later, they heisted Sam "The Girl" Lazes (he was called "The Girl" because he abhorred violence), who worked for Los Angeles bookie Abe Benjamin and was kicking up to Jack Dragna. Their take was three grand. Benjamin called Dragna, who called Jimmy to a meeting at the Five O'Clock Club, owned by mobster Nick Licata.

As Dragna sipped a yellow Italian liqueur called Strega (the witch), he told Jimmy. "You know, Jimmy. These guys are no good. They have no respect, and they don't care whose toes they step on. The way I see it, we've got to clip them."

Jimmy took a gulp from a can of Acme beer.

"How do you drink that shit?" Jimmy told Dragna. "I can smell it from across the table."

"Forget about my drink," Dragna said. "Get rid of these two fucks. I want them gone."

"No problem," Jimmy said. "I have a great idea on how to set them up."

On the evening of October 7, 1951, Jimmy had learned from Sam Lazes, that the two Tonys were set to meet Lazes at the apartment of Sam London, a movie extra and a friend of Jimmy's. The purpose of the meeting was for Lazes to give the two Tonys five grand, as a token of his friendship. When the two Tonys showed up at London's apartment, Jimmy was there instead of Lazes.

Jimmy offered his hand to Tony Trombino, but Trombino just looked at Jimmy's hand like it was holding a dog turd.

"What gives here!" Trombino said. "We're here to see that other guy."

"We've got to talk," Jimmy said.

London gave each of a three men a beer, and then he evacuated his own apartment, just in case. The three men sat around the kitchen table and nursed their beers.

Jimmy knew Brancato better than he knew Trombino, so directed his speech to him.

"Listen Tony, Sam Lazes is with some good people," Jimmy said. "He's with Abe Benjamin who's a good friend of mine."

"Sorry, Jimmy, but we need this cash," Brancato said. "We got a robbery case in Las Vegas, and we need money for a lawyer."

"But this guy Lazes is a broken down valise," Jimmy said. "He's got no money like that. So you can forget that, right off the bat. But there are other ways to get you that money."

"Yeah, like what?" Trombino said.

"There's this card game tonight," Jimmy said. "It's on Broadway. You guys can take it for ten, maybe even fifteen grand."

"If it's such a good deal, why aren't you doing it yourself?" Trombino said.

"Yeah, Jimmy," Brancato. "You don't need us for something like this. I heard this was your specialty in Cleveland."

Jimmy took a sip of beer.

"I ain't in that racket no more," Jimmy said. "I'll set it up for you, and bring you a set of tool (guns), and I get a full cut. One third of the take."

"Well, even if we agreed to do this, we'd need at least one more guy," Brancato said.

"No problem," Jimmy said. "I'll bring in one more man, and I'll drive the getaway," Jimmy said. "Listen, I said ten or fifteen grand, but this is a high stakes game. There could be forty-fifty grand there for the taking."

Brancato looked at Trombino and nodded. Trombino nodded back.

"Yeah, this sounds good," Trombino said. "And we sure need the fuckin' dough."

Jimmy told them the place where they would meet in two hours.

"Like I said, I'll bring the tools," Jimmy said. "You just bring the car."

Jimmy rushed to Jack Dragna house and told him the deal. Dragna decided that Charlie "Bats" Battaglia would be the other shooter, and Angelo Polizzi would drive them to the meet, which was scheduled to take place at Hollywood Boulevard. Jack Dragna provided the guns, two .38 caliber pistols.

At ten minutes before the scheduled meeting. Polizzi dropped off Jimmy and Charlie Bats on Hollywood Boulevard. He parked two blocks away on the same street, where he would have a clear view of the festivities. Leo Moceri, a mobster from Cleveland, sat in a car behind him - the crash car - which Moceri would crash into any car, police or otherwise, who tried to follow Polizzi's car after the shooting. Jimmy had already arranged for an alibi at a downtown bar, where a waitress was ready to swear he had been there all night.

As they stood waiting for the two Tonys car, Jimmy and Charlie Bats both had their guns stuffed down the front of the waistbands and covered by button-down sweaters. Jimmy noticed Charlie Bats' face was a sickly light gray.

"Relax," Jimmy told Charlie Bats. "This will be over in five seconds. Remember, when they pull up you get in the back seat first behind the driver, and I'll get in next to you. As soon as the door is closed, you cut loose. Hit the guy in front of you, and I'll take care of the other one. Then get out of the car and walk calmly across the street. I'll follow you, and Angelo will pick us up. You got it straight?"

"Yeah, I got it straight," said Charlie Bats, but he didn't sound too convincing.

"Just be calm and don't shoot yourself in the balls," Jimmy said. "That's what happened to Polack Mike, and he never fucked a broad again. And he lived in Vegas where there's a horny broad every two feet. What a fuckin' shame."

After a ten minutes wait, Jimmy spotted the two Tonys in a stolen car. Trombino was driving, and Brancato was sitting next to him.

"Okay, it's Showtime," Jimmy told Charlie Bats.

They hustled over to the two Tonys' car. Jimmy opened the back passenger door. Charlie Bats got in first, which put him behind Trombino. Jimmy got in next to Charlie Bats, putting him behind Brancato. Before anyone said a word, Jimmy pulled out his gun and started blasting away; the first two bullets imbedded themselves in the back on Brancato's head. Jimmy turned to Charlie Bats who was frozen with his gun in his right hand.

"Shoot, you motherfucker!" Jimmy yelled.

All Charlie Bats could manage was a moan.

As Trombino tried to flee the car, Jimmy quickly emptied the rest of his bullets into the back of Trombino's head. It was only then that Charlie Bats got the guts to fire his gun. And that he did, once time. The bullet ricocheted off the side of Trombino's head and exited the car through the front window.

Then Charlie Bats, with no prodding from Jimmy, pushed open the car door and ran across the street. Jimmy followed close behind, walking quickly and shaking his head, trying to stop the reverberations in his skull caused by guns firing in contained quarters.

After dropping off Charlie Bats, Polizzi drove Jimmy home. He took off all his clothes and handed them to Polizzi, who rushed out to burn the clothes at a convenient location. The, Jimmy took a shower, making sure to scrub his hands and under his fingernails to remove traces of the gunpowder. In 1951, paraffin tests for gunpowder were in their infant stages and were not perfected yet.

Jimmy wondered how he was going to break the news to Jack Dragna about the cowardice of Charlie Bats. Jimmy knew some men can handle hits, and others shit their pants when called upon to step up to the plate and do the right thing. Jimmy also knew, if Dragna knew the truth, there was a good chance Charlie Bats could get executed for his failure to perform.

Jimmy decided to go to sleep and worry about Charlie Bats later.

Just before 6 a.m., there was a loud banging on the front door of Jimmy's house. Jimmy's wife, Jewel, awoke first. She shook Jimmy, who was deep in slumberland.

"Jesus, it not even dawn yet," Jewel said. She saw a face at her bedroom window. "Jimmy, there's people outside. What's going on?"

Jimmy slipped his legs over the side of the bed.

"Don't worry about it," he told his wife. "It's probably the cops breaking balls again."

Jimmy's brother, Warren, who had left Cleveland and was living with Jimmy and Jewel, ran into Jimmy's bedroom.

"Jimmy, I hope it's the police outside, because if it's not, we're in big trouble," Warren said.

Jimmy smacked Warren on the side of the face; just hard enough to get his attention.

"Fuckin' calm down, will ya?" Jimmy said. "It's probably nothing. I'll take care of it."

Jimmy calmly opened the front door, and the police blasted in like gangbusters. Jimmy figured there were enough cops to arrest a small platoon.

"Hey, you guys got a warrant?" Jimmy said. "You just can't come busting in here like that."

The lieutenant in charge just smirked.

"We don't need a warrant, scumbag," he said to Jimmy. "We arresting you and you brother for murder."

"My brother?" Jimmy said. "Warren wouldn't even kill a fly."

Ignoring Jimmy's remarks, the cops slapped the cuffs on Jimmy and Warren. But not before they let Jimmy phone a doctor for Jewel who had fainted at the sight of the police invasion.

The police lieutenant stood next to Jimmy as he made his phone call. Jimmy looked over his shoulder at the lieut.

"What the fuck are you looking at?" Jimmy said. "How about a little privacy?"

The lieutenant smiled.

"I'm just making sure you call a doctor and not your lawyer," he said.

"Ain't I entitled to a lawyer?" Jimmy said.

"Maybe in Cleveland where you come from?" the lieutenant said. "But you're in Los Angeles now. We do things different."

"I bet you do," Jimmy said. "I bet you do."

Los Angeles Police Chief William H. Parker had been waiting for a moment like this for a long time. With Cohen languishing in jail, and with Jimmy not having a political rabbi like Senator Arthur Samish, Chief Parker had anointed Jimmy Los Angeles' Public Enemy No. 1.

The murder of the two Tony's had made front page of the newspapers, not only in Los Angeles, but in tabloids all across the country. The photo of the two Tonys dead and bloody in the front seat of their car had even been plastered on the national news television programs as far away as New York City. Chief Parker knew that arresting a high profile mobster like Jimmy Fratianno would make him the poster boy for law enforcement all across the country. And if the charges stuck, Chief Parker saw himself as the potential mayor of Los Angeles and possibly the future governor.

As soon as Jimmy and Warren were booked in the local police station, Chief Parker ordered his men to take the two brothers to the Ambassador Hotel, where Parker could captivate the press with his sensational allegations.

On the morning of October 8th, 1951, Chief Parker stood at the podium at the Ambassador Hotel and told the assembled press, "I believe we have the man who engineered the murders of Tony Brancato and Tony Trombino."

Standing next to Chief Parker on the podium was Police Captain James Hamilton who wanted a chunk of the glory too.

"The chief means we have the triggerman or the mastermind behind the shootings," Captain Hamilton said. "His name is Jimmy 'The Weasel' Fratianno."

Captain Hamilton went on to say that the "slayings were tied to a smashed southern California bookie empire and the legal bookmaking empire in Las Vegas."

Captain Hamilton claimed that "Jimmy Fratianno had become the alleged successor of gambler Mickey Cohen."

Captain Hamilton then dropped a verbal bomb on Jimmy when he said, "We have in custody a witness who saw the killer's face."

But he declined to give the witness's name for "obvious reason."

Chief Parker literally pushed Captain Hamilton to the side, so that he could make the bold announcement that, "The underworld went too far this time. This was a sloppy killing. We will break this case soon, and with it, other gangland killings."

Because witnesses had said they had seen Jimmy on the night of the double murder in Nick Licata's Five O'Clock Club, Licata was brought in for questioning. After Licata said Jimmy had been in a club from 7 p.m. until closing, Licata was arrested too as an accomplice in the murder. The police then put out a warrant for Angelo Polizzi and Charlie Bats, as well as for Dago Louie and Louie "Lips" Moceri. All were arrested, questioned, and held over for a later appearance before a grand jury.

At this point, it was obvious that the Los Angeles police wanted a conviction in this case, and let the law be damned. That would come back to haunt them later.

After the press conference, Jimmy was summoned to a third floor suite at the Ambassador Hotel. Up to this point, Jimmy had refused to answer all questions and had repeatedly asked to see his lawyer. For some reason, the police, against the law of this land, told Jimmy he had no rights to see his lawyer, unless, that is, he signed a full confession.

When Jimmy entered the third floor suite, he spotted Chief Parker and Captain Hamilton, sitting on the couch. They directed Jimmy to a chair opposite them, and as soon as Jimmy's rump hit the seat, they began peppering Jimmy with questions. Jimmy made believe they were invisible, and he was deaf.

Finally, Jimmy said, "Hey, what's going on around here? I want my lawyer. What is this place, Russia? I know my rights, and I want to see my lawyer now."

It was Chief Parker's and Captain Hamilton's turn to play deaf.

"You know why you're here, Fratianno," Chief Parker said. "We know you killed Tony Brancato and Tony Trombino, and we have an eyewitness who saw you do it."

"Your eyewitness is full of shit," Jimmy said. "Oh, and by the way, did I mention I want to see my lawyer?"

Chief Parker's face turned red. He jumped from the couch and hovered over Jimmy. Jimmy figured he was about to get tuned up (beat up), which was a common Los Angeles police interrogation tactic. But all Chief Parker did was bellow into Jimmy face, his spittle flying up into the air and across Jimmy's forehead.

"You think you're pretty smart, don't you Fratianno?" Chief Parker said.

Jimmy wiped the spittle from his forehead with the back of this hand. He smiled, and said, "Only compared to the people in this room. Sitting here, I feel like fuckin' Einstein."

Chief Parker took a step back, and then he jumped forward again, his mouth close enough to Jimmy's face he could have bitten off his nose without moving.

"We know all about you Fratianno," Chief Parker said. "We've known for years. We know you're a Mafia hitman and behind a lot of the murders around here in recent years. And if it's the last thing I do, I'm going to nail you, Fratianno. I'm going to take that smug look off your face, and when they fry your ass at San Quinten, I'll be there to wave good-bye. What do you have to say about that?"

Jimmy smiled, and said, "I say you'll fry in the electric chair before I do. And I still want to see my lawyer."

The next day, Jimmy was dragged before the grand jury. He still hadn't seen an attorney, but he knew his rights. He refused to answer every question given to him by the prosecutor, Adolph Alexander, citing the Fifth Amendment protecting a citizens from self-incrimination.

Five days later, Jimmy and all the other defendants were released on bail.

The grand jury convened for seven weeks, and it was the over-exuberance of the Los Angeles Police department that sunk their case.

The waitress at the Five O'clock Club was summoned before the grand jury. This was the same waitress who had originally said Jimmy was at the Five O'clock Club the entire night of the double murders. But under brutal police questioning, she changed her story and said that Jimmy had snuck out and disappeared for at least two hours.

On the stand, the waitress dropped a bombshell on the prosecutionwhen she said, "The reason I changed my story was that two detectives came to my apartment. They burned me with cigarettes on my breasts and my buttocks, places where the marks wouldn't show, until I changed my story and said Jimmy wasn't at the Five O'clock Club all night long on the night of the murders. The truth is Jimmy was there all night.

During the waitress's testimony, District Attorney Alexander looked like he was ready to puke. He had no choice but to dismiss all charges, and he directed the Los Angeles Police Department's Internal Affairs division to look into the matter of the two detectives behaving badly as far as the Five O'Clock waitress was concerned.

Predictably, it was "she said," and "they said," and no charges were ever brought against the detectives in question.

As soon as the charges in the two Tonys' murder case evaporated, Jimmy "The Weasel" Fratianno was as happy as a witch working in a broom factory. Not only was he cleared of all charges, but the name "Jimmy the Weasel," which had previously been know only in mob circles, was famous throughout the country. Being of limited intelligence (his prison I.Q was 96), Jimmy thought this was a good thing; the American public now knew Jimmy "The Weasel" was a big shot and possibly a killer. This meant enhanced adoration and better service at restaurants, and better seats for the fights at the Olympic Auditorium. Mickey Cohen was once the darling of the Los Angeles media, but now Jimmy had inherited that mantle, and it fit just fine as far as Jimmy was concerned.

Jack Dragna became more impressed with Jimmy after he done in the two Tonys, and rubbed it in the face of the Los Angeles Police Department. In February 1952, Dragna decided to induct new blood into his Los Angeles crime family. Dragna selected Joe Dippolito's vineyard as the site of the induction, knowing quite well that Frank Niccoli resided permanently on the premises, six feet under some of the best grapes in sunny California.

The men to be inducted were Angelo Polizzi, Charlie "Bats" Battaglia (Jimmy never did tell Dragna about Charlie Bats' stage fright on the night of the two Tonys' hit), Carlo Licata (son of Nick Licata), Joe Dippolito himself, Joe LiMandri and Joe Adamao.

When the ceremony was finished, and the newluy made men made the round kissing cheeks and "amico nostra-ing" everyone in sight. Then Jack Dragna did something very strange and totally unexpected. He called for quiet, raised his glass in a toast, and asked Jimmy "The Weasel" Fratianno to sit on his right side, the place of honor for the family's *caporegime*. This shocked everyone in attendance, but especially Nick Licata, who had been close to Dragna for many years and had expected to be elevated to that post himself.

"I'm making Jimmy Fratianno my *caporegime*," Dragna said. "Are there any objections?"

No one said a word, not even Nick Licata. But it was obvious that Licata and several of the men present resented that Jimmy, who had only been in Los Angeles for five years, be awarded such a high honor.

Jimmy didn't know it, but on that day he made some enemies who would hurt him later in life.

Jimmy's next "piece of work" concerned Frank Borgia, who was Jack Dragna's San Diego bookmaker, and who also was in Jack Dragna's doghouse . Dragna had soured on Borgia, because Borgia complained he was being shaken down by Gaspare Matranga. What Borgia didn't know was that Dragna was a partner with Matranga in the shakedown. So, as far as Jack Dragna was concerned, Borgia had to go.

Dragna issued the contract to Jimmy, and Jimmy enlisted his old friend and stone killer, Frank "Bomp" Bompensiero, to help with the planning of Borgia's demise. After Bomp came up with a plan, Jimmy met him at Bomp's restaurant in San Diego - The Gold Rail.

Bomp and Jimmy sat at a table in the back of the restaurant, munching on Italian cold cuts and Italian cheeses washed down by an aged Chianti. Jimmy was especially impressed with the imported prosciutto and capicola.

"Damn Bomp, this stuff is good," Jimmy said. "Where did you get it from?"

"I get this 'pro-shoot' straight from the old country," Bomp said. "It has to be certified and everything by the Italian government. And stamped too by the Italian meat inspectors. I pay almost five bucks a pound for this stuff, but it's the real McCoy. Now, the 'gabagool' is imported too, but I get it after it falls off a few trucks up north."

"Well, I guess Frank Borgia is down to his last good Italian meal," Jimmy said. "What's the plan?"

Bomb chugged down three fingers of Chianti from a lead crystal wine glass.

"We're going tonight," Bomp said. "I've got Tony Mirabile to set him up. He's Borgia best friend, so Borgia won't suspect a thing. Tony's taking him to Joe Adamo's house tomorrow, and we'll be waiting there with the rope."

While the two men chowed down, Carlo Licata, Nick Licata's son who had just gotten his button joined them at the table.

Bomp got right to the point.

"We're taking out Frank Borgia tomorrow night, and we need you to dig a hole." Bomb said.

Carlo looked like he had just been smacked in the face.

"Have you checked this out with my father?" Carlo said.

"Hey, check what out with your father? What are we running a Sunday school here?" Bomp said. "Jimmy here is your captain, and he calls the shots, not your father."

"That's right, Carlo," Jimmy said. "You just got made, and you have to follow orders, you know that. Your father has nothing to do with this. But if he were here, he'd tell you the same thing. Orders are orders."

Carlo left the table, dragging his tail. He drove to where Bomp said the hole had to be dug, and he commenced digging until the hole was six feet deep.

Around 8 p.m. the following night, Tony Mirabile knocked at the front door of Joe Adamo's San Diego house. With him was his pal, Frank Borgia.

Jimmy opened the front door, smiling.

"Hey guys, come on in," Jimmy said. "Joe's in the living room."

Borgia entered first, and as soon as was totally inside, Bomp kicked the door shut.

Immediately, Mirabile grabbed Borgia in a bear hug from behind, while Jimmy slipped the rope over Borgia's head. Bomp grabbed the other end of the rope, and both men pulled with all their might for a full 60 seconds. When they were sure Borgia was dead, they let loose of the rope and Borgia fell flat on his face, dead as stone.

Joe Adamo and Tony Mirabile put Borgia's corpse in a body bag they had gotten from a local funeral home. Then they dumped the bag into the trunk of Mirabile's car. Mirabile drove, with Adamo as added muscle, to where Carlo Licata had dug the hole for the body's disposal.

After Mirabile pulled away, Jimmy and Bomp sat at the kitchen table.

"It was sad to see old Frank go," Bomp said. "But we did what we were ordered to do. Case closed."

Bomp went to the refrigerator and brought out a bag filled with imported Italian cold cuts and cheese. He and Jimmy commenced eating with both hands. And instead of wine, they washed down the delicacies with canned beer.

"You know, Jimmy, you've got to be careful with Jack Dragna and his brother Tom too," Bomp said. "And I don't trust Tom's son, Louie, as far as I can throw the Golden Gate Bridge. With these guys, thing's aren't always like you think they are. It's like a crooked card game. The hand is quicker than the eye, and when they deal seconds, they bury you."

"Yeah, I got the same feelings that you've got," Jimmy said. "I don't get them making me captain instead of Nick Licata. It don't make sense. Maybe they're looking to set me up. Get my confidence, and then clip me."

"We've both been around," Bomb said. "We know how it goes, so it's better if we both watch each other's back."

'Yeah, and I heard there's a chance they are going to bump you up to capo, too," Jimmy said. "Then they'll have us right where they want us."

"Keep your eye on that fuckin' Louie Dragna," Bomp said. "I had to give him a piece of the Gold Rail because his uncle said so. And Jack's son, Frank, has got a piece too. So the Dragnas own two-thirds of my joint. We might be 'amico nostra' to them, but remember blood is thicker than water. When push comes to shove, the Dragnas will eat us alive."

"Fuck them all," Jimmy said. "Let's eat."

In late 1951, Jack Dragna started sending Jimmy Fratianno back and forth from Los Angeles to Las Vegas to keep his eye on the Outfits gambling interests, and especially Dragna's end of the bargain. Vegas was also where several national Teamsters officials, including upstart Jimmy Hoffa, and the Outfit's top mobsters, especially Outfit capo Joey Glimco, met to decide who would be selected and not elected as the top Teamsters officials throughout the country.

In April of 1953, Jimmy was in Vegas on Teamster business when he got the contract to take out Louis "Russian Louie" Strauss, who was once charged with the murder of his partner, Harry Sherwood, when they both owned The Bar of Music in Reno. Since witnesses were nowhere to be found, eventually the charges against Russian Louie were dropped.

Russian Louie, a handsome devil and a degenerate gambler to boot, made most of his money as a gigolo. When Jimmy got the contract to clip him, Russian Louie was milking big- time cash from the lovely Mickey Smith, a knockout blond who ran the card room in the Barstow Hotel, which she also owed. Smith's boyfriend was Big Bill Bonelli, a crooked California politician who controlled the issuance of state liquor licenses. But the love of her life was Russian Louie.

Although Russian Louie was a lot of things, and most of them not-so-nice, his downfall began when he decided to blackmail gambler and Las Vegas casino owner, the cowboy hat-wearing Benny Binion. Binion was a three-time killer himself, who was only convicted twice; both times in Texas. After Binion moved from Texas to Las Vegas, he opened the Westerner Gambling House and Saloon. In 1951, Binion bought the Eldorado Club and the Apache Hotel, where the Eldorado Club was located. Then he changed the name of the gambling joint to Binion's Horseshoe Casino.

All the gambling licenses were under Binion's name, which was slightly illegal because of Binion's previous murder convictions. Russian Louie knew this, and he stared bleeding Binion dry, under the threat of revealing Binion's history in Texas to the Nevada Tax Commission, which was the body who issued gaming licenses before the 1959 creation of the Nevada Gaming Control Board. What Russian Louie didn't know was that Binion was tight pals with Jack

Dragna, who got an illegal kickback from Binion's Nevada casino earnings.

When he got tired of paying Russian Louie, Binion reached out to Nick Licata, who in turn relayed Binion's predicament to Jack Dragna. Dragna replied by saying, "Okay we can handles this, but what are you going to do for us?"

Binion replied by saying that as soon as Russian Louie was no more, Binion planned to build another casino on a vacant in the "Glitter Gulch" section of downtown Las Vegas. Binion said that he would give Dragna 25% of all the profits, including the skims. Dragna said fine. But then there was the little problem of a National Crime Commission edict that no dead bodies could be found in the state of Nevada, because they didn't want to kill the goose that laid the golden egg by pissing off Nevada law enforcement.

Dragna gave the contract to Licata, but Licata was an old man and not as capable as either Jimmy Fratianno or Frank Bompensiero in the killing department. The contract was placed in Licata's hands in October of 1951, and after fiddling around with idea after idea about how to kill Russian Louie, by April of 1953 Russian Louie was still alive and still blackmailing Binion for hundreds of thousands of dollars a year.

So, Dragna finally did the smart thing: he transferred the contract to Jimmy Fratianno. Marshall Caifano and Phil Alderisio were brought in from Chicago to assist Jimmy in Russian Louie's demise. This Midwestern support could only happen with the permission of the top mob boss of Chicago, which by this time was Tony "The Tuna" Accardo. The Tuna gave a fins-up decision, and Caifano and Alderisio traveled to Las Vegas where they hooked up with Jimmy Fratianno.

The problem was that Fratianno had never met Russian Louie, but Marshal Carfano had. So, it was up the Caifano to make the introductions so that Jimmy could get close enough to Russian Louie to kill him without raising any suspicions beforehand.

On April 16, 1953, Russian Louie was in a pickle. He had just blown a ton of cash at the craps tables on the previous night, and he needed an infusion of cash to settle up his markers. Marshall Caifano found Russian Louie at a casino bar at around noon, and Russian Louie was not looking too chipper. With Caifano was Jimmy "The Weasel" Fratianno.

"Hey Louie, how you doing?" Caifano said.

"Not too good," Russian Louie said. "I was up all night crapping out at the tables."

Caifano introduced Russian Louie to Jimmy.

As he eyed a huge diamond ring on Russian Louie's right pinkie that could choke a gorilla, Jimmy said, "How bad did you bust out?"

Jimmy later discovered this ring was a present to Russian Louie from his paramour, Mickey Smith.

"Twelve grand worth," Russian Louie said. He turned to Caifano. "Do you think you could loan me a few bucks to pay my tab?"

"How much?" Caifano said.

"Twelve thousand bucks," Russian Louie said. "The casino's holding my marker for ten grand. If you can't do twelve, at least I need the ten."

"Gee, I wish I could help you out, but I just got in from Chicago," Caifano said. "I don't have anywhere near that kind of cash with me."

"Maybe I can help you out," Jimmy said. "This guy owes me twenty grand, and he's holding out on me. He's in Upland, California, and if you help me collect, I'll front you the twelve grand, at only two points a week vig. I usually charge five, but Marshall is your pal."

"Sounds good," Russian Louie said. "When do we go?"

"Right now," Jimmy said. "The faster I get my money, the faster you get the twelve grand."

"Sorry guys, but I already got plans," Caifano. "But Phil Alderisio is in town. I'll see if he can make the trip with you."

"Okay," Russian Louie said. "But I got to make a stop at my place to pick up some clothes. I've been in these duds for the last two days, and I'm starting to smell like a gorilla."

Jimmy patted Russian Louie's on the back.

"Good idea," Jimmy said. "We have a long drive ahead of us, and I don't need you stinking out my car."

After making a phone call, ostensibly to the fictitious man who owed him the twenty grand, Jimmy, driving his dark green Cadillac convertible with Russian Louie sitting next to him, picked up Phil Alderisio from a local motel. All three absconded to Russian

Louie's apartment on the outskirts of town. While Russian Louie went to his apartment for a shower and a change of clothes, Jimmy and Alderisio stood outside in Jimmy's car.

"Hey Phil, you drive and I'll sit in the back," Jimmy said.

When Russian Louie arrived back at the car, Jimmy directed him into the front passenger seat. Jimmy was especially annoyed that Russian Louie's diamond ring was not on the pinkie finger of his right hand. Jimmy had planned to snatch the ring after Russian Louie's last breath.

"I'm going to take a little nap," Jimmy told Russian Louie.

And that Jimmy did, while Alderisio did all the driving.

More than three hours and 240 miles later, Alderisio pulled in front of a sprawling ranch-style house located in Upland, a suburb of San Bernardino, at the foot of the tallest part of San Gabriel Mountains.

"Phil, you go inside collect for me," Jimmy said. "He's expecting us."

Phil entered the house, and when he didn't return in five minutes, Jimmy faked concern.

"I don't know what's keeping him," Jimmy told Russian Louie. "Let's go inside and find out what's going on."

Jimmy knocked on the front door, and Joe Dippolito answered the door. Russian Louie had never seen Joe Dip before in his life, and he wouldn't see him again, either.

Joe Dip reached out his right hand to shake Russian Louie's hand, and when he had a firm grip, he pulled Russian Louie through the front door.

Frank Bompensiero had the rope ready, and as soon as Joe Dip had Russian Louie in a reverse bear hug, the festivities started. Bomp wrapped the rope around Russian Louie's neck, and he handed the other end of the rope to Jimmy. While Jimmy and Bomp strangled the life out of Russian Louie, Charlie Bats, Angelo Polizzi, Louie Dragna and Gaspare Matranga all emerged from the living room, and they watched in awe as the two pro killers did what they did best.

After everyone had a celebratory drink, Joe Dip and Angle Polizzi dropped Russian Louie's body in an already-dug hole at the bottom of the San Gabriel Mountains. Then they filled in the hole with dirt.

Russian Louie's remains were never found.

A few months later, when it was obvious Russian Louie was no longer of this earth, Mickey Smith bugged the Las Vegas police so much that they had to start an investigation into his disappearance. The Las Vegas cops went through the motions (Benny Binion had most of the Las Vegas cops, including the Chief of Police on his pad), and they questioned the usual suspects, which included Jimmy the Weasel and Frank Bomp.

"Sorry, I don't know the man (Russian Louie)," Jimmy told the cops.

"Me neither," said Frank Bomp.

That concluded the investigation into the disappearance of Russian Louie.

"Boy, that Mickey Smith is a knockout," Jimmy later told Bomp. "And she's loaded with cash. Now that Russian Louie is gone, I'd like to get my hooks into her."

"Forget about it," Frank Bomp said. "Her boyfriend is Big Bill Bonnelli (the head of the California State Board of Equalization). If I had his cash, I'd burn mine. The broad gets her money from him."

"Well, she went for Russian Louie, didn't she?" Jimmy said. "What did Russian Louie have that I don't?"

"Besides him being ten times better looking than you, probably nothing," Frank Bomp said.

Jimmy "The Weasel" Fratianno spent his entire life making money dabbling in illegal activities with people connected to the underworld. Jimmy had strenuously avoided the so-called "legal deals," where the "legitimate" people you did business with, if caught doing something not exactly kosher, would rat out their own mothers. So, when Jimmy was approached with a legitimate oil deal, where Jimmy could legitimately invest $5,000 in return for one third of a two percent stake in the 435-acre oil leasehold in Ventura County's Tapa Canyon, he was skeptical.

But Jimmy agreed to listen anyway.

The Terry Drilling Company held this leasehold, and Jimmy was told they were looking for additional investors. The owners of the company were George Terry and Carl Riddell. Two of Jimmy's old pals from Cleveland, Jimmy Modica and Dom Raspona, had already invested four grand in the leasehold. They wanted to bring Jimmy on board. Jimmy knew that both men had been involved in illegal activities in Cleveland, but in California they were strictly known as successful liquor store owners.

Modica and Raspona visited Jimmy in his Encino home and laid out the proposition.

"Jimmy, this is a great deal," Modica said. "This joint has already drilled its first hole, and there's oil just gushing out of it."

"That's right," Raspona said. "And Jimmy, if you get involved with just a five grand investment, me and Jimmy Modica will personally guarantee your investment; even if it means we have to dig into our profits from our liquor stores. We're putting up four grand of our own money, and the nine grand investment will give us two percent of the profits."

"Why am I so lucky you guys are bringing me into this sure thing?" Jimmy said. "You guys are doing alright, and you certainly don't need my five grand."

"We like to do favors for the right people, in case we need favors in the future," Modica said.

This deal sounded too good to me true to. And if Jimmy had listened to his instincts, he would have told Modica and Raspona to get lost. But Jimmy was flush with cash. And in fact, he was leaving the next day on a cross-country trip, first to see the Kentucky Derby in Louisville, and then to the Ohio State Penitentiary, in Columbus, to visit his old chum, Yonnie Licavoli, the man who had done Jimmy so many favors in the past. Also on Jimmy's itinerary was a trip to Detroit to attend the wedding of Carlo Licata, Nick's son, to Josephine Tocco, the daughter of Black Bill Tocco, the second in command to and brother-in-law of Joe Zerilli who ran the Detroit branch of the Italian mob.

After mulling it around in his brain for a few moments, Jimmy decided, why not? So, he reached into his pocket, pulled out a roll of bills, peeled off $2,500, and handed it to Modica.

"I'm leaving first thing in the morning," Jimmy told the two men. "Come by tomorrow, and my wife will get the other $2,500 from the bank."

Jimmy stood to shake hands with the two men. He squeezed Raspona's hand in a vice-like grip.

Jimmy told him, "Remember this is a legitimate deal, and I want the legitimate contracts drawn up to prove my investment."

"No problem," Raspona said.

Jimmy knew whenever someone said "no problem," problems were sure to follow.

Jimmy was out of town for three weeks, and when he returned he had some good news and bad news waiting for him.

The good news was that the Terry Drilling Company had struck oil in Tapo Canyon; eight times to be precise. Terry was presently pumping eight bountiful wells, which produced enough oil to make everyone involved very rich men.

According to an article in the *Los Angeles Times*, the estimated value of the Terry Drilling Company's strike was a staggering eighty million dollars. Jimmy consulted the calculator in his brain, and he came up his, Raspona's, and Modica's two percent now being worth $1.6 million. Whack that up three ways, and Jimmy was sitting on over a half a million dollars profit on an investment of five grand.

Nice work if you can get it, and as far as Jimmy Fratianno was concerned, this money was his; no if, ands or buts.

However, the main problem was that Terry and Riddell claimed they never even heard of Jimmy Fratianno. And worse, Terry was saying he never consented to any two percent deal with either Raspona, whom he did know, nor Modica, whom Riddell said he knew as well as he did Fratianno; which was not at all.

Terry later testified in court, "I knew Mr. Raspona for four years, and in all that time I only had one business dealing with him, and that was in 1950, when I leased an oil rig to him."

On February 20, 1953, Terry said, at Mr. Raspona's request, he visited Raspona at his liquor store in Burbank.

"When I met Mr. Raspona at his liquor store, he asked me if I knew of any royalties for sale in the Terry Drilling Company's Tapo Canyon wells," Terry said. "I told his there was a Mr. Lopspeich who had a two percent overriding royalty and that he might be interested in selling. I checked into the matter, and a few days later I told Mr. Raspona that Mr. Lopspeich was not interested in selling. Mr. Raspona told me that was too bad, because there were 'some very fine people' who wanted to buy some royalty in the well."

Jimmy Fratianno had a different take. He told several mob friends at a get-together in his Encino home, "These two guys, Terry and Riddell are trying to fuck me. We tried to arrange a meeting to straighten things out, but these guys are being cute. The minute they struck oil, they gave Raspona my money back, trying to pull a fast one. These so-called legitimate oil guys are all thieves. But this jerk Terry is real stupid if he thinks he can get away with this shit. He picked on the wrong guy this time."

If Jimmy had just accepted the fact he was being fucked, the matter would have ended right there. After all, he did get his five grand back, so what did he really loose?

Jimmy figured, even though he didn't know Terry and Riddell from the man in the moon, he was losing respect. And to wiseguys like Jimmy respect was everything; not to mention the half-a-million bananas Jimmy figured was rightfully his.

And that's when Jimmy Fratianno got stupid.

First, Jimmy told Raspona to get in touch with Riddell, who had no clue what was going on, and tell him, "These people mean business. These people will blow your and Terry's and my head off if you did not make contact with Terry and straighten the thing out. These people have a 'network' all over the country, and there will be lots of trouble if this contract isn't made and this so-called deal completed."

Raspona did what he was told, and he added to Riddell, "You better arrange a meeting with yourself and Terry and these people, or they will blow your head off. And if you go to the cops, you're a dead man too."

Raspona figured he was a dead man either way, so he contacted the local police and, to the delight off Jimmy's old nemesis, Captain James Hamilton of the Los Angeles Police Department, the law installed a bug on Riddell's office telephone. The bug in place, Riddell told Terry to contact Raspona, and to tell him to have Jimmy Fratianno call Riddell's office number and to do it from a pay phone. Riddell told Raspona that both Riddell and Terry wanted to straight this out. And that they will both be in the office when Fratianno called.

Jimmy did what Carl Riddell requested, and the taped telephone conversation went as follows:

> *Fratianno: Carl, I want to be a man with you and a man with George Terry. Now this has gone far enough. We put up our money. People are talking. Now I ain't going to stand for it. Now, I'm going to tell you another thing. As far as Terry is concerned I don't give a flying fuck! People can go to the police all they want. The police is not going to watch him 24 hours a day, 365 days a year.*

> *Riddell: Yeah.*

> *Fratianno: If the motherfuckers go to the coppers about me, they're going to die. I'll tell you right now, I'm plenty mad. I want to be a man, and I want that other cocksucker to be a man, because his motherfuckin' money ain't going to do him no good when he's dead. Now you tell him. You put him on the phone with me, Carl. You tell Terry I want to talk to him. Will you put him on the phone?*

Carl Riddell handed the phone to George Terry.

> *Fratianno: Let me tell you something, Terry. Now we're not going to get fucked on this thing. You know that, don't you?*

> *Terry: I didn't know I had any deal with you.*

Fratianno: Well, I had a deal with Dom (Raspona) and you had a deal with Dom. Is that right?

Terry: I started the deal with Dom , and then I told him that the deal was off.

Fratianno: You did tell him? Well, look Terry. It's not off with me, and I'm going to tell you one fuckin' thing and I don't give a shit who knows it, coppers or no coppers. I'll blow your motherfuckin' head off. I'm going to tell you right now, you ain't fuckin' with no kids.

Terry: Well, I never met you in my life.

Fratianno: And you ain't going to meet me. You don't have to meet me, Terry, because you ain't going to know me. And I'm going to tell you, you'd better straighten this fuckin' thing out, and straighten it out fast. I'm going to give you one fuckin' week to straighten it out, and if you don't straighten it out in one fuckin' week, you cocksucker, you could have people following you the rest of your fuckin' life. And I'll blow your fuckin' head off. All your money ain't going to do you no fuckin' good. You, Carl and Dom straighten this fucking' thing out and straighten it fast. Now put Carl back on the phone.

George Terry handed the phone back to Carl Riddell.

Fratianno: Okay, Carl. I told Terry I'm going to give him seven fuckin; days to straighten this thing out. I don't give a fuck who he goes to, understand? I've been talked about enough as it is in this fuckin' town. I've had enough heat and I'm not going to get any fuckin' more. Now get ahold of Terry and Dom and straighten this fuckin' thing out.

Riddell: I'll do the best I can. What else do you want me to do?

Fratianno: That's all.

Riddell: Will you hurt my family?

After hearing Riddell's remark about Jimmy hurting his children, it finally dawned on him that maybe this conversation was taped.

Jimmy went stone silent.

Riddell: Are you still there?

Fratianno: Yeah, Carl, will you do that for me?

Riddell: I'll do the best I can.

Fratianno: Okay, good-bye.

As soon as Jimmy Fratianno put down the receiver, he knew he had just stepped on his own dick.

The next day, Jimmy told Jack Dragna, "I never mentioned hurting this guy's family. I never hurt a kid or a woman in my life. Why did he bring it up unless he wanted to get me on tape."

"It look's bad," Dragna said. "Those guys must have gone to the coppers and put a recorder on that phone. That's why they asked Raspona to give you that phone number."

"Yeah, and this means the deal's down the drain too," Jimmy said. "Well, I'll be a son-of-a-bitch. I knew better than to get involved with these legitimate cocksuckers."

Two days later, as Jimmy was driving his green Cadillac convertible in Fairfax on his way to San Diego to pick up money owed to him by a San Diego bookie, a state patrol car pulled him over to the curb. Jimmy was searched, handcuffed and arrested, and taken to the Los Angeles county jail. As Jimmy was being booked, a lieutenant from Police Captain James Hamilton's Intelligence Division was all smiles.

"Jimmy, the boss wanted me to tell you he's got you dead-bang this time," the lieutenant said.

Jimmy smirked.

"Tell Chief Hamilton to go fuck himself," Jimmy said.

"Maybe he will," the lieutenant said, smiling. "But not until after he finishes fucking you

While in the local jail, Jimmy Fratianno knew things were going south for him when he read statements in the newspapers, attributed to him, that we not only false, but he would have to be a moron to have said them.

His old foe, Chief Parker, told the press that when he was arrested Jimmy had boasted, "I'm the Weasel. I belong to a very powerful organization. You read a lot about it in the newspapers."

Chief Parker also told the press the crux of the extortion charges was that Jimmy had told Carl Riddell, "My organization, which has headquarters in Denver, will get you no matter where you go."

Jimmy knew that a good fellow named Vinnie Colletti was the boss of the Italian mob in Denver, but Jimmy had never met Colletti. And up until that time, Jimmy had never visited Denver, not even to gawk at the bison at the Rocky Mountain Arsenal. Jimmy later discovered that a distant cousin of his, Ray Lanese, had, in fact, uttered this threat while impersonating Jimmy in a phone call to both Terry and Riddell, which was set up by Dom Raspona without Jimmy's knowledge or consent.

Raspona was also arrested in the extortion plot, along with James Modica. All three men were released on $100,000 bond, which, adjusted for inflation, would be one million dollars in 2014 money.

The trial of the three men started in early August of 1953, and after his first day in court, Jimmy was dismayed to discover that his bail had been revoked, and he was ordered to stay in prison all during his trial. However, Raspona and Modica, who had made dozens of threatening calls to both Terry and Riddell, whereas Jimmy only made one phone call, were allowed to return home every weekday night during the trial and all day on the weekends.

Jimmy lawyer, William B. Beirne, tried to get Jimmy released on a Writ of Habeas Corpus, but on August 13, a superior court struck down that writ.

Chief Parker, again trying this case in the court of public opinion, praised the ruling of the superior court. He told the press that Fratianno had threatened Terry and Riddell by saying, "You know about our organization; I know you've read about it. So you know there is no way to get away from this. On the other hand, if you take us into the company, you have nothing to worry about."

Chief Parker added, "As a result of Fratianno's threats, we have both the Terry and Riddell family under 24-hour protection.

When Jimmy read Chief Parker's remarks in the newspapers the following day he was livid. He told his attorney, Beirne, "These guys are making it up as they go along. I said a lot of things in that one phone call, but I never said what that cocksucker Parker said I said about 'our organization.' I'd be a moron to say something like that."

The trial started in mid-January of 1954 and lasted more than two months. On March 17, 1954, it took a jury of eight men and four women only four hours to come in with guilty verdicts on all three charges of extortion for Jimmy Fratianno, 40, Dominick Raspona, 41, and James Modica, 46. Judge Ralph K. Pierson set March 24 as the date for hearing the defense attorney's motions for a new trial.

Those motions were denied, and on April 7, 1954, Judge Pierson laid down the hammer on Jimmy Fratianno.

Even though Raspona and Modica initiated the entire Terry Drilling Company fiasco, and even though they were much more active in threatening both Terry and Riddell, on the phone and in person, they were both given only $2,000 fines and absolutely no jail time. Jimmy was not fined a cent, but Judge Pierson hit him with a five-to-fifteen year jail sentence.

At sentencing, attorney Beirne told Jimmy, "Don't worry, I have Tom Hiller writing up an appeal right now. Five-to-fifteen is a joke. At most you'll serve two, two and a half years."

As his appeal was being prepared, Jimmy was sent to the gloomy Folsom State Prison in Represa, California; a level II prison which also has a minimum security prison just outside the main gate. Though his appeals attorney, Tom Hiller, Jimmy found out that the Los Angeles Police Apartment had added an addendum to his Case Summery Report.

It said: "Police records indicated Subject has been known to have a hand in selling narcotics on a large scale."

Jimmy did his time at Folsom working in the vegetable garden, which gave him daily access to fresh air. While he was in prison, Jimmy found out that his old mob pal, Frank "Bomp" Bompensiero, had been convicted of the bribery of Big Bill Bonelli, for illegally obtaining two California state liquor licenses; one for Bomp' Gold Rail in San Diego, and one for the Pirate's Cove, who Bomb also owned, but was presently "out of business."

The key witness against both Bomp and Bonelli was Mickey Smith, who had set up the connection herself. The scuttlebutt said that Smith was especially angry at Bomp, who she knew had something to do with the disappearance of her boyfriend, Russian Louie. As for her long-time benefactor, Bonelli, he had already cut off Smith's cash flow. But by this time, her Las Vegas gambling houses were raking in so much dough, Smith needed Bonelli like she needed rabies. So, it was bye-bye Bonelli, and screw you Bomp; you're both going to jail. Bomp got three to forty two years and a $15,000 fine. He did five years at San Quentin State Prison before being released on May 14, 1960.

Big Bill Bonelli did have the last laugh, of sorts, over his ex-paramour, Mickey Smith. When the indictments came down, Bonelli absconded across the California border to Mexico, where he spent the rest of his life living in the luxury the millions of dollars in kickbacks he had extorted could afford him.

In 1956, Jimmy's appeal attorney, Hiller, was able to get Jimmy sentence reduced to one-to-ten years. Hiller also had a pal in Assemblyman Lester McMillan, who for the under-the-table sum of twenty-five thousand dollars got Jimmy transferred to Soledad Prison, which was more like a vacation resort than a prison.

Jimmy later told Frank "Bomp" Bompensiero, "It was the best twenty five grand I ever spent."

It was later alleged in a 1969 *Look Magazine* article that this twenty-five grand made its way into the hands of California Governor Edmond G. Brown. It was Jimmy's ex-son-in-law, Thomas Lee Thomas, who had told *Look* that he had seen Jewel Fratianno wrap up the twenty-five grand in paper on her kitchen table. Jewel later told Thomas that she delivered the money herself to Governor Brown in Sacramento.

"The transfer (to Soledad) came through shortly afterwards," Thomas told *Look*.

Jimmy, now in his early 40's, took advantage of the athletic fiends at Soledad, where he played both softball and basketball, when he wasn't working on his suntan on the grass in the common outside areas. In the evening, Jimmy played dominos and checkers, and his mental as well as his physical well-being improved exponentially.

In December of 1959, Jimmy was transferred to San Quentin, where he had to undergo skin grafting on his chest after the removal of several nasty keloids. The first person to meet Jimmy when he got off the prison bus, was Frank "Bomp" Bompensiero, who was five months from his prison release date. Jimmy arrived with a few boxes of his favorite cigars, and Bomp displayed a few boxes of his own.Bomp personally checked Jimmy into the hospital ward, making sure to tell everyone in sight what a big man Jimmy "The Weasel" was.

One night, Bomb asked Jimmy if he could bring Jimmy a man named Chuck Cahan to his hospital bed for a visit. Cahan had done Jimmy wrong a few years back by paying another thug, Jack Whelan, $5,000 to give Jimmy a beating. Instead, Whalen tipped Jimmy off to the deal, and he split the $5,000 with Jimmy. Jimmy had been looking for Cahan ever since.

"Why the fuck would I want to see that piece of shit?" Jimmy told Bomp.

"I'll tell you why, because Cahan works for and is in tight with the top priest in the joint," Bomp said. "If you give Cahan assurances he won't get hurt when he gets out in a few months, he can pull some strings with the priest in here to put in a good word at your next parole hearing."

Jimmy smiled, and said, "That's a damn good reason as any for meeting Cahan. So set it up."

The next night, Bomp bought Cahan to Jimmy's prison bed. The men shook hands, and smoked a few cigars together.

"So, you and I are okay now?" Chan said.

"We are if you can get that priest to write some nice shit in my prison report," Jimmy said.

At the Jimmy's next Adult Authority's Parole Review, Cahan's pal, Catholic chaplain Father John Dingberg, put the following note in Jimmy's Parole Release Referral Report:

"Although subject has been at this institution but a short while, at the time of this report, he has contacted the writer for help with various problems and has demonstrated an interest in a fulfillment of his religious obligations. He accepts his circumstances in an intelligent manner and evidences a sincerity of purpose toward the future. When not confined in the hospital, the subject has attended Mass and his contact with the writer has demonstrated appreciation of all efforts made on his behalf."

On July 14, 1960, exactly two months after his pal, Frank "Bomp" Bompensiero was sprung from the can, Jimmy was granted parole. However, as a condition of his parole, Jimmy could not meet with any of his old mob cronies, and was restricted by law to the pint-sized northern California town of Redding - 1960 census population of 12,773. Redding is 200 miles north of San Francisco and 500 miles north of Los Angeles; hardly a stone's throw from Jimmy's

Jimmy's parole officer, Carl Roggi, was not too sure Jimmy would remain on the straight and narrow. He wrote in his pre-sentencing report:

"The writer questions the ability of any officer to adequately supervise an individual such as Fratianno. This man will, no doubt, cause us considerable trouble and will require the strictest type of supervision that we can exercise at this or at any other time. Any mismanagement of facts and circumstances could easily embarrass our good parole system. We must be guarded at all times."

Being on such a short lease, Jimmy did the smart thing – he went totally legit. By September, Jimmy, through Teamsters Local 137, obtained a job at the Riley Trucking Company. Jimmy bought himself a truck, and he was paid $10 an hour for hauling various materials from warehouses to construction sites.

To help put food on the table, Jimmy's wife, Jewel, studied hard, and she obtained a real estate license under the name "Jewel Farrell." Jewel soon got employment at the Dom Cram Real Estate Company as a "real estate saleswoman."

Just because Jimmy was restricted in his travel, did not mean he would actually observe those restrictions. While he was in jail, Jimmy's tight buddy, Jack Dragna, passed away, and with Jimmy not available to influence such things, Frank DeSimone became the new boss. DeSimone anointed Nick Licata as his underboss. Both men despised Jimmy, and while he was in prison, Jimmy's bookmaking and shylocking businesses were absorbed by the new West Coast mob hierarchy. Jimmy also discovered, through Frank Bompensiero, that DeSimone, to keep Jimmy out of his hair, put out a contract out on his life.

The only person Jimmy could trust was Jimmy Roselli, and after work on an early Friday afternoon, Jimmy quietly left Redding in his two-year-old Ford and made the nine-hour trip to Los Angeles. Jimmy made sure he stuck to the speed limit, lest he be pulled over by state cops and sent back to the slammer.

Bomp had told Roselli that Jimmy was on the way, and Roselli set up a secret 11 p.m. meeting at a swanky restaurant located on the top floor of a new high rise office building on

Wilshire Boulevard. Jimmy dressed properly for the occasion, but he was somewhat surprised when he was met at the front door of the restaurant by the maître d who was wearing a brilliant black tuxedo.

After dispensing with the small talk, Roselli, dressed to the nines as usual, leaned across the table, and he said in almost a whisper, "What's this problem you have with Nick Licata?"

Jimmy took a long sip of scotch which was married nicely in a crystal tumbler with two ice cubes.

"Johnny, when I went into the can, I had $100,000 on the street in shylock money," Jimmy said. "I gave my book to Charlie Bats and told him to run it like he saw fit, and just to take care of Jewel and my kid. Well, he took care of Jewel alright. He gave her a measly $150 a week. This went on for about six months until Jewel told me about it. Then Louie Dragna tells Jewel that Charlie Bats lost all my money on the streets and wasn't that just too bad."

"I heard it was more to it than that," Roselli said.

"Yeah, there was. So you know about it too?" Jimmy said.

"Things like that get around," Roselli said. "You know that."

"It's fuckin' infuriating, but I was in the can, so what could I do?" Jimmy said. "Jewel told me that one time when Charlie Batts was delivering the money to her, he tried to rape her, but she fought him off. The money stopped right after that."

"So what did you do?" Roselli said. "That's one solid rule of our organization – hands off the wives of other members."

"I told Jewel to go see Jack and Tom Dragna and tell them what had happened," Jimmy said. "She did, and they called that ugly fuck Charlie Bats on the carpet. So, obviously he lies and says it never happened. Charlie Bats said Jewel was just trying to make herself look important. What could I do? I had another six years to do in the can. So I let it rest, until now."

"Let me tell you something," Roselli said. "When Jack died, I got myself transferred back to Chicago. This was after this prick, DeSimone, told me he was elected unanimously. How could that be? I never got a chance to vote. Did you?"

"That's bullshit!" Jimmy said. "DeSimone came to Soledad to see me about who should be the new boss, and I told him you were the best and most logical choice. Then he went to visit Bomp in San Quentin and Bomp told him the same thing. So how could the vote have been unanimous?"

"Well, I'm happy I'm back in Chicago," Roselli said. "I'm with Paul Ricca, the main guy. And his underboss is Sam Giancana, another swell fellow. Fuck those pricks in California."

"What does Chicago have you doing these days?" Jimmy said.

"Sam asked me to concentrate on their interests in Las Vegas," Roselli said. "They had plenty of cash to invest in some gambling joints. I'm the man in Vegas now. I got the Stardust for Chicago."

"Then that's it," Jimmy said. "I want to get transferred back to Chicago to be with you and those guys. At least they are honorable men. Maybe they'll sent me out to Vegas to work under you."

"Yeah, you're right," Roselli said. "That's the right move for you. But before I check this out with Chicago, let me run it past Tommy Brown (Luchesse) in New York City. But don't worry. Both Tommy Brown and Sam Giancana know the good work you've done in the past. There should be no problem."

A few weeks later, Roselli sent a cryptic message to Jimmy in Redding, and using the codename Shamus, the message said, "The weather was beautiful in New York and in Chicago. I just completed a most enjoyable and successful trip."

Unfortunately for Jimmy, the weather in Redding turned out to be quite lousy.

Working for somebody else was just not in Jimmy Fratianno's makeup. After toiling for short money with the Riley Trucking Company, he decided to quit. That meant that Jimmy's parole officer, Craig Wright, would get his underwear all bunched up in a ball unless Jimmy got himself another job. To satisfy Wright, Jimmy went into business for himself. And it was all perfectly legitimate.

Jimmy's Redding contact in the Teamsters Union was Duane Wemple, who was informed of Jimmy's V.I.P. status by the Teamsters bosses in the Midwest, including Teamsters president Dave Beck and his second-in-command, Jimmy Hoffa. Wemple told Jimmy if he could line up 40 truckers or more to work for Jimmy, Wemple would guarantee Jimmy all the work his truckers could handle. Figuring each truck would earn around $100 a day, and with Jimmy taking five percent off the top, Jimmy was looking at a cool $1000 a week profit, just to act as a middleman between the truckers and the union. With assistance from Wemple, Jimmy had no problem getting 40 union truckers to work for him at his new business, the Fratianno Trucking Company. In addition to subcontracting the work out to his union truckers, Jimmy also drove a truck himself for 10 hours a day, five days a week

To increase his bottom line, Jimmy decided to work all ends of the spectrum. His truckers would need gas for their rigs, so Jimmy leased a gas station with an eight thousand gallon tank. The gas, including the tax, would run Jimmy about 20 cents a gallon, and he'd sell it to his truckers for 25 cents a gallon. Truckers are also in constant need of tires, oil, fan belts, and repairs. Jimmy made deals with several wholesalers to take care of all his trucker's needs, with Jimmy taking five percent of the top. In addition, Jimmy hired his own mechanic to maintain the trucks of his union truckers, plus his own trucks.

In six months' time, Jimmy, busting his hump in the trenches, was raking in a mint. This did not please Jimmy's former employer, Charles Riley Jr., the owner of the Riley Trucking Company. Riley started making complains about Jimmy to the FBI, the local sheriff's department, and knowing Jimmy was on parole, to the Adult Parole Division. The main gist of Riley's complaints was that Jimmy was a known member of "organized crime," and that Jimmy's connections in the underworld made Riley fear for his life.

The complaints traveled up the administrative ladder, and soon Carl Roggi, the District Adult Parole Division supervisor, whose office was in Sacramento, paid Jimmy a little visit in Redding.

"I'm afraid I've got bad news for you, Jimmy," Roggi said. "You're going to have to relocate out of Redding."

"What for?" Jimmy said. "I'm running a legitimate business. I bet Riley has something to do with this."

"Yes, the Rileys have said you're running them out of business," Roggi said. "The Rileys are natives of this community. They're going around saying that a notorious gangster is responsible for them losing so much money they might have to close up shop. Plus, they told the FBI that your 'connections' are making them nervous about their future health."

"What am I in, Russia?" Jimmy said. "I'm doing everything by the book, and now you're running me out of town."

"Remember Jimmy, you're on parole." Roggi said. "You have limited rights. As long as you are on parole the Adult Parole Division can tell you where you have to do your time. That's the law in California."

"But the way I'm going, I can net fifty grand a year," Jimmy said. "And it's all legitimate."

"Sorry Jimmy, the decision is already made," Roggi said. "I'm relocating you to Sacramento."

Jimmy put forth every persuasive argument he could think of, but it was to no avail.

It was "Sacramento, here I come" for Jimmy Fratianno, and Jimmy lost no time in turning a negative into a positive.

In Sacramento, Jimmy rented a duplex for him and Jewel in a residential neighborhood (While he was in San Quentin, Jimmy's daughter, JoAnne, married Thomas Lee Thomas. They relocated to Sacramento to join Jimmy and Jewel in the Fratianno Trucking Company.) Jimmy parked his six trucks at a local service station, where he maintained an office. And through local Teamster connections, Jimmy was quickly able to get work for all his six trucks, including the one Jimmy still drove 10 hours a day.

With Jewel and Joanne working as dispatchers, the Fratianno Trucking Company, by tapping Jimmy's contacts in the Teamsters, started moving 50 trucks a day in the Sacramento area. The money was so good, Jimmy invested the profits by buying six transfer unit trucks, which were able to haul 25 tons a time. This allowed Jimmy, because of the large capacity of the transfer units, to undercut the truckers who owned the smaller capacity dump trucks. In all, Jimmy owned 12 trucks of various capacities and capabilities, and with money he derived from kickback schemes only a true criminal like Jimmy could devise (Jimmy made sure that money went on the books and that he paid taxes on it), the legitimate money was gushing in like pressured water from a fireman's hose.

But Jimmy Fratianno was nothing if he wasn't a gangster, and eventually he eased himself back into the illegitimate world, while still keeping a foothold in his trucking business.

Due to the intervention of Johnny Roselli, Jimmy was now officially with the Chicago Outfit. Jimmy's old crew in Los Angeles, and especially Louie Dragna, the late Jack Dragna's nephew, were not too happy with Jimmy's defection.

One day, Jimmy got a surprise call at home from Louie Dragna. Jimmy had no use for Louie Dragna since he knew Louie never did a "piece of work" in his life, and on top of that, he wasn't a good earner either. Louie Dragna was where he was, (in Jimmy's absence, Louie had been made a captain), strictly because he was Jack Dragna's nephew and the son of Tom Dragna. When he got Jimmy on the line, Louie told Jimmy to go to a specific phone booth and to call him back from that number. Jimmy did as he was told, but he didn't like it one bit.

As soon as Louie Dragna answered the phone, Jimmy tore into him.

"What the fuck are you trying to do?" Jimmy said. "You know I'm on parole."

"Long time no see, Jimmy," Louie said. "When are you coming down to visit your old buddies?"

"What are you deaf? I said I'm out on parole," Jimmy said. "I can't associate with certain people."

"Well yeah, that's funny," Louie said. "Then how did you get yourself transferred to the Chicago crew? Nick DeSimone and Frank Licata said you never spoke to them about it."

"Fuck the both of them!" Jimmy said. "They put a blanket on me; took all my street money when I was in the can."

"But how did you do it? How did you get transferred?" Louie said. "We heard that Johnny Roselli took care of everything for you."

"Hey, listen you cocksucker, why are you trying to get Johnny in trouble?" Jimmy said. "He was a friend of your father and your uncle. You know it's against the rules for him to get involved like that."

"Well, we just heard Johnny went to bat for you in Chicago," Louie said.

"Bullshit!" Jimmy said. "You're just trying to get Johnny in trouble."

"Listen Jimmy, Johnny got himself transferred to Chicago," Louie said. "He ain't with us no more, and we've got to look out for our own family."

"Well that's great, but I don't want anything to do with your fucking family," Jimmy said. "I went to see Sam (Giancana), and I got myself transferred. If you don't believe me, call Sam. Johnny had nothing to do with it. Now take it from there, you two-faced cocksucker!"

Finished venting, Jimmy banged down the receiver on the pay phone.

The first order of mob business Jimmy got involved with after being moved from the California crew to the Chicago Outfit was handling the Outfit's order to whack Desi Arnaz. Yes, that Desi Arnaz, the Ricky Ricardo of "I Love Lucy" fame.

Arnaz was a no-talent singer/bandleader who had the good fortune of marrying one of the most beautiful and talented woman performers ever - Lucille Ball. In 1951, the couple was set to star in what became one of the most popular television series of all time – *I Love Lucy*. The dominant star of the show was Lucille Ball, who had morphed from an actress in "B" movies (she was called "Queen of the Bs"), to one of the best comediennes of all time. The problem with *I Love Lucy* was that although Ball and Arnaz had been married since 1940, no producer would touch the show with the hammy Arnaz playing the straight man to the zaniness of Ball's comedic genius.

In 1950, Lucy, to protect Desi from being shit-canned by the producers, decided to start her own production company - Desilu Productions. She made Desi president of the company. Ball's contributions were mostly on the artistic side, and she left the business decisions up to her husband. The show debuted in 1951, and you can still see reruns of *I Love Lucy* on cable television networks.

The first run of *I Love Lucy* totaled seven seasons. In 1957, after the final *I Love Lucy* episode aired, Arnaz turned his attention to producing other shows. Arnaz went on to executively-produce *The Ann Southern Show* (1958), *The Andy Griffith Show* (1960), and *Star Trek* (1967).

What Arnaz didn't know was that he almost didn't make it to 1967.

Ball and Arnaz divorced in 1958, and as part of the divorce settlement, Arnaz remained as executive producer of Desilu. Ball was involved in Desilu Productions only as it applied to her own television career, which included *The Lucy Show*, which ran from 1962 to 1968.

In 1959, Arnaz executively-produced on ABC Television a controversial show called *The Untouchables*, which starred Robert Stack as federal crime-buster Eliot Ness. The storyline of the show was Ness and his boys, dubbed "The Untouchables" because the underworld was incapable of corrupting them, were intent on either putting "bad guys" in jail, or killing them in a hail of bullets.

Most of the "bad guys" in *The Untouchables* had Italian surnames, like Capone (played by Neville Grand) and Nitti (played by Bruce Gordon) - real life gangsters who had left this earth more than a decade before. (Capone, afflicted with syphilis, died of a heart attack after doing seven years in the Alcatraz Federal Penitentiary, and Nitti committed suicide before he was arrested for extorting the Hollywood Film Industry).

The show and its content went over like a lead balloon in America's Italian-American communities.

A group called the Federation of Italian/American Democratic Organizations picketed outside ABC's headquarters in New York, urging the sponsors of *The Untouchables* to withdraw their support of the program. These sponsors included the Liggett & Meyers Tobacco Company, which produced the very popular Chesterfield King cigarettes.

The Federation of Italian/American Democratic Organizations issued a statement to the press saying, "*The Untouchables* vilified Italian-Americans, stereotyping them as a singular criminal element."

The Untouchables especially pissed off one of the most prominent Italian/Americans in America, Frank Sinatra, who was great pals with Jimmy's new boss – Sam Giancana. Sinatra had his own production company on the Desilu lot, and after a heated argument with Arnaz, Sinatra moved his production company to a different lot. Witnesses said the argument became so heated; the two men almost came to blows. It didn't help that in the course of the argument, Arnaz reminded Sinatra that his television career had been a disaster.

To add more fuel to the fire, FBI Director J. Edgar Hoover, who was especially close to several New York City mobsters, including "The Prime Minister of the Underworld," Frank Costello (Castiglia), angrily contacted Desi Arnaz and told him to stop "invading former FBI cases," like Hoover claimed Arnaz did in a 1959 episode entitled "Ma Barker and Her Boys."

Hoover reminded Arnaz, that although Ness was a federal agent, he was not a member of the FBI. In *The Untouchables*, Ness was repeated referred to as a G-Man, which is a term that is specifically used for the FBI

In a scathing letter, Hoover wrote to Arnaz, "In the 'Ma Barker and Her Boys' episode, besides Ma Barker (played by Clair Trevor) referring to Ness as a G-Man, Ness also referred to a document his was using as an 'FBI fly sheet.' The impression is clearly conveyed that Ness is an FBI agent, when, in fact, he was not."

One morning in the spring of 1963, While Jimmy was in his Sacramento trucking company office, he got a phone call from "Shamus" who told him to be at a specific Sacramento phone booth in an hour.

Jimmy called "Shamus" from the designated booth, and Johnny Roselli told him, "Meet me at the Friars Club tomorrow at noon."

When Jimmy arrived at the Friars Club the following day, he was greeted not only by Roselli, but also by Sam Giancana, who was in town for a hotel room romp in the hay with a famous Hollywood starlet.

According to *The Last Mafioso* by Avid Demaris, after the three men enjoyed a scrumptious lunch, Giancana excused himself from the table, but not before he told Jimmy, "We've got something we want you to handle. Johnny will explain it to you."

Roselli picked up and paid the check.

Then he told Jimmy, "Let's go for a little ride along the coast. I have something I want to discuss with you."

As they passed through Malibu Beach in Jimmy's Ford Thunderbird, Roselli quipped, "You know, Ricky Riccardo has some spainlin' to do. He's pissing off the wrong people."

"Who the fuck is Ricky Riccardo?" Jimmy said.

Roselli smiled, and said, "I guess you didn't watch too much television in the can."

"Television? Who had time for television?" Jimmy said. "I was too busy dealing marked cards and rolling loaded dice. Television don't put no cash in my pockets.

With the sound of the waves blasting off the surf in the background, Roselli said to Jimmy, "Now that you're out on parole, have you seen that television show *The Untouchables*?"

"Maybe once or twice," Jimmy said. "I don't have time to watch that shit."

"Well, did you know that Mae Capone, Al's widow, filed suit against the show for millions in damages?" Roselli said. "Mae lost that suit, and things have gotten worse since."

"Nobody pays attention to garbage like that," Jimmy said. "It's like a comic book; a joke. Who cares?"

"I'll tell you who cares," Roselli said. "Sam cares. Paul Ricca cares, and Joe Batters (Tony "Big Tuna" Accardo) cares.

"I know that," Jimmy said. "But the general public could give a flying fuck."

"Jimmy, it's already been decided by our family," Roselli said. "And I've talked to Bomp about it. We're going to clip Desi Arnaz. He's the producer of the show."

"Well, what do you want me to do now?" Jimmy said. "Like you said, I'm still on parole."

"Jimmy, we might not even use you," Roselli said. "Talk to Bomp. We got two, maybe three guys coming in from Chicago. Make sure he's on the right track, and then go back home."

"Okay, but if you need me, call me the day before and I'll whip right down here," Jimmy said. "Remember, I'm available at any time."

Jimmy dropped off Roselli at the Friars Club. But before he got out of Jimmy's car, Roselli said, "Bomp will meet you at the grill at the U.S. Grant at 4 p.m. Work it out with him."

When Jimmy arrived at the grill at the U. S. Grant, Bomp was already sitting at a table, guzzling down Chivas and puffing on a huge Cuban cigar.

"Hey, Jimmy sit down," Bomp said. "Have a cigar."

Jimmy never refused a cigar, so he took one from Bomp and ordered Jack Daniels on the rocks from the waitress.

After some small talk about the state of affairs of the Los Angeles mob family (both Jimmy and Bomp agreed that after the death of Jack Dragna the group had no-balls-leadership), Jimmy told Bomp, "How are you set on this deal?"

"I cased his (Arnaz's) house in Del Mar, but I don't think he's in Del Mar right now," Bomb said. "But Johnny wants him hit in Del Mar and not in Hollywood where his studio is located. So, we have to wait until he gets back. I figure we hit him at night like we did on the Rummel job (In 1950, Sam Rummel, Mickey Cohen's lawyer, was shot and killed at night in front of his home on Canyon River Drive in Los Angeles by Angelo Polizzi. Jimmy was close by in a crash car)."

"What do you have for tools?" Jimmy said.

"I've got a couple of thirty-eights stashed with my barber," Bomp said. "But I want to use a couple of sawed-off shotguns. That way we can work in the dark, no problem."

"I can get them from Billy Graham," Jimmy said. "He's got a hell of a connection. They're not registered, clean, and brand new. You can drop them at the scene and nobody's ever going to trace them."

"Trace them or not, this is a fuckin' tough nut to crack," Bomp said. "You can't be hanging around Arnaz's house with the tools for three four hours at a time waiting for him to come home. You get caught with them tools and it's back to the joint. Frankly Jimmy, we're going to have to get lucky to hit this guy."

"Take my advice and let the other guys hold the tools," Jimmy said.

"If we can set it up and they send us only two guys, then I might need you to drive," Bomp said. "There's nobody here I trust for the job. I'll handle the crash car."

Two weeks later, Frank Bompensiero phoned Jimmy in Sacramento.

"It's all fucked up," Bomp told Jimmy. "The boys from Chicago got disgusted waiting by Arnaz's house, and they went back to Chicago. They said they'll be back, but I don't believe them. As far as I'm concerned the deal if off until I hear otherwise."

"So, what are you going to do?" Jimmy said.

"I'm going to sit tight and do nothing," Bomp said.

"Listen, if they ask me, I'll do it," Jimmy said. "But if you want my opinion, Sam Giancana had a cross-hair up his ass that day. I think he's already forgotten about it. As for Los Angeles, Sam just comes down here to get laid and count his money. This *Untouchables* shit will blow over."

Maybe Desi Arnaz heard there was a contract on his life (he went to high school with Al Capone's son, Sonny), or maybe it was just a coincidence. But days after the Chicago hit men went back to the Windy City, Desilu Productions sold the rights to *The*

Untouchables to ABC television, and Desi Arnaz sold his Desilu shares to his former wife, Lucille Ball. There was also the dirty little secret that each *Untouchable* episode cost Desilu $65,000 to $70,000 to produce, but ABC was only paying Desilu $65,000 to air each show. So, why would Arnaz risk his life for a show that was actually losing money?

The last first-run show of *The Untouchables* aired on May 21, 1963. Like *I Love Lucy*, reruns of *The Untouchables* can still be seen on cable television networks.

On April 7, 1964, after three and a half years on parole, the California state Adult Parole Division finally cut Jimmy loose.

In Jimmy's release from parole report, Agent Wilbur wrote: "Fratianno's case is notorious in the annals of the Adult Parole Division and with law enforcement throughout the state. Numerous allegations have been made against the Parolee and all have been checked out with results showing the Parolee to be clean. He has many good qualities and this has been brought out in many dealings with people he does business with. Unless some unfortunate circumstances should arise, Parolee should continue as a successful businessman and a good citizen."

Jimmy "The Weasel" Fratianno had pulled the wool over the eyes of law enforcement again.

Now, since Jimmy could talk and meet with whomever he pleased, Jimmy could reach for the stars in the underworld, while maintaining the outward appearance as the honest owner of a trucking company.

The first problem Jimmy had after he was released from parole was with his wife, Jewel. Jimmy had drummed it into Jewel's head that she must never discuss the Fratianno Trucking Company business with outsiders in the room. One night, Jimmy invited Frank LaPorte, a Chicago capo, and his wife, Harriet, to dinner at their Sacramento home. Jewel was hitting the bottle pretty good, and she started getting mouthy and arrogant. Her beef was with Jimmy advancing thirty-five hundred dollars to an independent trucker, who was slow paying the money back.

With LaPorte and his wife within earshot, Jewel told Jimmy, "That money you loaned that guy, you can kiss that money goodbye. I knew he was a deadbeat the moment I saw him."

Jimmy put his right forefinger to his lips

"Be quite, let it lay," Jimmy said.

Jewel was obviously half in the bag. She hissed at Jimmy, "Yeah, you, Mr. Bigshot, you got taken by a little punk."

Now it was Jimmy who raised his voice.

"You better shut up, you're drunk!" Jimmy said. "If you want to talk about money, talk about the money I've earned for this business. Never mind the thirty-five hundred. How about the three hundred and fifty thousand that's in the bank? Legitimately. Talk about that, goddammit!"

Jewel got right up in Jimmy's face.

"I'm the president of this company and if you want to throw away your money, it's fine," Jewel said. "But don't go to Joanne and ask her to sign checks for the company. That's my money you're throwing away."

"I'm telling you for the last time, stop your yapping," Jimmy said. "We have guests in the house."

"This is my house, and I'll talk all I want," Jewel said.

As a reflex action to being talked to in such a manner, Jimmy smacked the whiskey glass out of Jewel's hand, and the glass fell to the floor.

"Don't pick it up if you know what's good for you," Jimmy said. "I've never hit a woman, but there's always a first time. Now go to bed. Get out of my fucking sight!"

Jewel left the living room and climbed the stairs to her bedroom.

Seeing Jewel leaving in distress, Frank LaPorte came into the living room.

"Your wife is drunk," LaPorte said. "Cut her some slack."

"Fuck cutting her some slack," Jimmy said. "This is what happens when you take a housekeeper and make them president of a fucking company."

A few days later, Jewel filed for divorce, claiming "extreme cruelty" on Jimmy's part.

What Jimmy didn't know was that on the very day of his argument with his wife, Jewel had a secret lunch with an unscrupulous FBI agent named Clarence Newton, who was looking to put Jimmy back in jail.

As was told by Michael J. Zuckerman in the book on Fratianno *Vengeance is Mine*, Newton had been failing for months to get Jewel to turn on her husband, with whom she was having on-again, off-again battles over various things, but especially the Fratianno Trucking Company.

Newton told Jewel, "That husband of yours is giving you a royal screwing. While you've been working yourself to death, he's been having a grand old time with several little girlfriends he has on the side."

"That's a bunch of bullshit!" Jewel said, nearly in tears." I've known this man for thirty-seven years, and there's no way he'd treat me that way."

Newton reached into the breast pocket of his suit jacket and pulled out a photo of Jimmy with his arm around a beautiful young blond, maybe 20 years Jewel's junior. The picture was taken when Jimmy had slipped way for hot weekend with the unidentified woman at Harrah's Tahoe.

"I tried to warn you," Newton said. "But this is what's he's been doing behind your back."

Jean stared at the picture for a few seconds, and then she stormed from the table without saying goodbye.

Jewel and Jimmy continued working and living together for a while. But after Jewel faked suicide by allegedly taking an overdose of pills in her bedroom, Jimmy had seen enough. He moved into a bachelor apartment on Robertson Boulevard. They still maintained a business relationship at Fratianno trucking; Jewel was still the president and a very capable bookkeeper.

But as far as Jimmy was concerned, he was loose and definitely on the make.

For the next few years, the Fratianno Trucking Company was raking in the business. Then Jimmy decided to do something very stupid.

Frank ReCupido, like Jimmy, owed a successful trucking business in Sacramento. ReCupido approached Jimmy about a huge windfall they could make together, working as sub-contractors for Miles and Company in the stifling hot dusty town of El Centro, just ten miles from the Mexican border.

At first, Jimmy was not interested

"What are you kidding me? El Centro?" Jimmy told ReCupido. "The mosquitos in El Centro are so big they could play linebacker for the San Francisco 49ers."

"Listen Jimmy, this is a huge deal." ReCupido said. "Miles and Company has the contract for transporting two million and a half tons of earth that they need for the construction of a freeway bypass in El Centro."

The ReCupido told Jimmy the big lie.

"And the Miles Company is paying the drivers by the hour," ReCupido said. "At the California Public Utility Commission (PUC) rate of $14 an hour, we'll both make a mint."

It cost Jimmy $20,000 to relocate his trucks from Sacramento to El Centro, which was 600 miles away. After just one month on the job, Jimmy was in the hole for $15,000. It seemed that Miles and Company was not paying the standard PUC rate of $14 an hour, but instead it was paying Jimmy and ReCupido 24 cents a ton. The drivers got 30% of the gross, but then Miles and Company, in order to satisfy state and federal regulations, converted the driver's pay into hours. It turned out that the drivers, who were busting their hump in dusty and stifling conditions for ten hours a day, while swatting away the swarm of mosquitos, were only getting paid 75% of what they should have been getting paid.

All of a sudden, Jimmy's five percent commission of his drivers' gross income was not looking so good.

So Jimmy decided to put the bull on Dick Mason, the truck boss for Miles and Sons.

Jimmy busted into Miles office, roaring at the top of his lungs, "What the fuck is going on here? You guys think you'll get away taking me for a jerk? I was promised the hourly rate by Frank ReCupido when I agreed to do this job; not 24 cents a fucking ton!"

Mason did not appear too impressed with Jimmy argument or reputation.

"If ReCupido told you that, he's a fucking liar," Mason said. "How could we pay an hourly rate on this kind of a job? The truck drivers just won't break their asses to get the job done quickly. It's just human nature. If we paid by the hour, we'll wind up taking it up the ass."

"What the fuck are you talking about?" Jimmy said. "My drivers are waiting sometimes as long as a half hour just to get loaded. The lines at the pits are more than a mile long, and my guys are dying from the heat. It must be 200 degrees in the cabs of my fucking trucks."

"That's another problem – the drivers," Miles said. "Some of them are taking breaks; drinking cokes and beers. Some are even taking time off to get laid. There's no way we can pay by the hour."

"Getting laid in this shithole town?" Jimmy said. "What are they fucking - the bed bugs? Besides, you must know you're violating PUC regulations."

Mason smiled, and said, "Everybody violates PUC regulations. We could never survive if we didn't. You know that. I bet you've violated them a million times yourself."

"Yeah, maybe," Jimmy said. "But I've never been fucked like this, and I'll tell you as nicely as I can, I don't plan to get fucked any longer."

Mason stood from his desk.

"Come on, let me take you to the Airport Inn for some lunch and a few drinks," Mason said. "I have an idea how to bail us both out. Plus, they have air conditioning at the Inn. We can think straighter without all the heat."

Jimmy soon decided that the best thing about the Airport Inn was the beer and the air conditioning. Jimmy and Mason both imbibed several micheladas, which is Mexican beer laced with lime juice, tomato juice, Worchester sauce, and chili powder, and served in 20 ounce mugs.

"You have to try the tamales here," Mason said. "They're the best in town."

Jimmy shook his head.

"I've been here a month, and I still haven't has a decent meal," Jimmy said. "Even the so-called Italian restaurants serve Mexican-style food."

"Jimmy, what do you expect?" Mason said. "Your five minutes from the Mexican border."

"Fuck the food, let's talk," Jimmy said. "What's your plan to stop me from getting fucked in this deal?"

"Jimmy, have you ever thought about selling your trucks to your drivers on conditional sales contracts?" Mason said. "That way you can list them as owner/operators and dispense with all the red tape, like unemployment, Workman's Comp, social security – all that shit. This would really simplify your operation."

"Yeah, I've been thinking about doing that for a long time," Jimmy said.

"Well, then do it," Mason said. "You can get the standard contracts at Crossland's Office Supply."

"Yeah, but these cocksucking drivers won't go for it," Jimmy said. "They're quitting on me left and right. They hate this fucking town."

"Well, we'll give them a reason to stay," Mason said. "We'll tell them as soon as this work is completed. I have a gravel haul that is easy work. You can bid on the whole thing, loading and hauling. I guarantee you the job, as long as your bid is reasonable."

"Okay, that might work," Jimmy said. "But look me in the eye and understand I'm not a guy who can get fucked twice. Understand?

"Absolutely," Mason said.

Mason waved to the waitress, "Two more micheladas, please; for me and the gentleman."

A few days later, Jimmy invited all his drivers to his air conditioned hotel suite at the Padre Trail Inn. Also present was Kenneth Bentley, Jimmy's site supervisor and crack truck mechanic.

Jimmy's chief go-fer, bone-breaker, and alleged foreman, Nick "The Greek" Diacogianis, was busy handing out cold beers to all the drivers, when Jimmy walked into the suite dressed to the nines and smoking a huge Cuban cigar. This wasn't the best image Jimmy could have projected before he hit his truckers with the hammer.

"You guys having a good time?" Jimmy said.

Nick the Greek cracked open a can of beer and handed it to Jimmy. Jimmy took a slug.

"Hold it down a bit," Jimmy said. "How would you guys like to own your own trucks and tractors; be owner/operators instead of getting fucked all the time?"

James Garrett was a new driver who didn't mind giving Jimmy some guff.

"Well, you're the guy who's fucking us, so why should we trust you?" Garrett said. "Besides, most of us are broke. How can we buy a rig that cost thirty to thirty-five thousand dollars?"

"That's the beauty of the thing," Jimmy said. "Nick is going to hand out conditional contracts that are all filled out already. All you have to do is sign them. You don't have to give me any money up front. When you have enough cash saved to make the down payments, I have contacts in the banks who will finance the loans for you, no questions asked. Then after the loan is paid, the rigs are all yours."

Garrett took a contract from Nick the Greek. He read it a bit, and then he sneered.

"Hey what does this mean?" Garrett said. This says that 'The driver agrees to lease the tractor exclusively to the Fratianno Trucking Company. Driver and tractor are to be under complete control of the Fratianno Trucking Company Buyer agrees to work whenever and wherever jobs are offered by the Fratianno Trucking Company.' I think that sucks!"

"Listen Garrett, what kind of moron do you think I am?" Jimmy said. "You think I'm going to sell you a rig on a conditional contract, and then watch you split with my money? I ain't that stupid."

Jimmy threw his lit cigar at Garret's feet.

"Listen if you don't want to sign the fucking contract, don't sign it!" Jimmy said. "You're a fucking slacker anyway; always late for work. Go find another job if you don't like my deal."

All the drivers present signed the documents, even Garrett who signed the following day. But the deal turned out to be so bad, both for the drivers and for Jimmy, within a month the drivers all quit and Jimmy went back to giving them their old deal back as on-the-clock workers.

However, Miles and Sons, including Dick Mason, never got the memo.

Miles and Sons continued to write the paychecks for the drivers who had signed the conditional contracts, even though those drivers had voided those contracts, with Jimmy's approval. Jewel and Joanne, back in Sacramento, were oblivious to what was going on in El Centro. While doing the payrolls, they still listed the drivers as "piece meal" workers, paying them according to Miles and Sons' guidelines, which dropped their pay scale from the required PUC standards of $14 an hour to $3.78 an hour.

As for Jimmy, he made the nine-hour trip in his new Caddy on I-8 from Sacramento to El Centro once a week. He never stood more than two days at a time and always at the best motel suite in town - the Padre Trail Inn, - which had air conditioning in addition to access to the hottest-looking hookers west of the Rio Grande and south of Los Angeles. Jimmy's favorite was a beaut named Sandy, who spent many hours of quality time on her back in Jimmy's suite.

When he was not engaged with Sandy, Jimmy met Frank Bompensiero, Leo Moceri and Frank LaPorte at his suite. And between dealing with the booze and the broads, they whacked up the shylocking money that Jimmy was bleeding from his own drivers, at up to five points (percent) a week. As for Frank ReCupido, who got him in the El Centro mess in the first place, Jimmy rewarded ReCupido by given him a job as his main shylock in town.

The roof began to cave in for Jimmy and his mob buddies when Nick "The Greek" Diacogianis had the bad grace to perpetrate an assault on James Garrett that propelled him into the El Centro slammer.

Nick the Greek's main job was to make sure the workers showed up for work on time. Because of the stifling heat, Nick decreed that his drivers arrive no later than 6:30 a.m., which allowed them to knock off around 4: 30 p.m. The real heat didn't kick in until around 10 a.m., so the first few hours of work were bearable for the drivers. However, James Garrett would not toe the line, and he rarely showed up for work until 8 a.m. Nick relayed this to Jimmy who told Nick to fire Garrett the next time he showed up late for work.

Sure enough, the day after Nick had received Jimmy's orders to fire Garrett if he were late again, Garrett showed up at 8 a.m.

"That's it Garrett, you've been warned and now you're fired!" Nick told him. "Give me the keys to your rig."

Garrett flung the keys at Nick's head, screaming, "I'm going down to the union hall and make a complaint. You guys don't know who you're fucking with!"

According to Nick, five minutes later, Garrett exited the union hall and headed straight towards Nick.

When Jimmy visited Nick in jail to arrange bail, Nick told him, "I see him coming back at me with his hands in his pocket. You know, that's the way they come at you with a shiv in the joint. So I popped him in the mouth, and he went down. Then he gets up and starts running away towards the police station. I run after him, and I see him rush up to two cops who were walking towards the union hall. So I turn around and take off in the opposite direction. But where can you hide in this fuckin' town? The cops caught me and threw me in jail."

Jimmy shook his head.

"Nick all you had to do was run into the police station and tell them your side of the story," Jimmy said. "Now, they are going to believe him instead of you."

Nick the Greek being in jail turned out to be the least of Jimmy's problems.

Only July 7, the *Imperial Valley Press* in El Centro published on its front page, the headline:

MAFIA PRESENT IN VALLEY

The story said:

"The Mafia is reaching its tentacles into the Imperial Valley. The Bomp, the Weasel and Nick the Greek have taken up residence in El Centro. They are operating Fratianno Trucking Lines Inc., which is engaged in hauling dirt for the new freeway being constructed across the southern edge of the county.

It has been reported that Fratianno's firm had sole a 1965 International Harvested tractor-truck to driver James Garrett for $16,500. The payments were $477.91 a month. A percentage of the payments for each load of dirt transported was to be applied to the monthly payments.

It was reported that is a driver did not stand for 'complete control' he can lose his truck and all that he put into it. Garrett says he was beaten by Nick 'The Greek' Diacogianis when he showed independence. Including Garrett's truck, four trucks have been repossessed in El Centro by Fratianno Trucking Lines Inc."

If the article had ended right there, it would have been bad enough for Jimmy and his mob pals. But then the *Imperial Valley Press* got to the real issue: mob control in their fine town.

"The Mafia follows a pattern when it moves into a new area. It uses legitimate business cover and soon starts to obtain 'control.' One of the 'controls' the Mafia is seeking is that of 'all trucking operations from San Francisco south.' They have boasted that 'control' is also sought in local government. The Mafia has that in Calumet City and to a large extent in Las Vegas."

After the *Imperial Valley Press* in El Centro started the ball rolling, every newspaper in California played up the California Mafia angle.

On Thursday, August 18, 1966, the *Eureka Humboldt Standard,* located in Eureka, which is 290 miles north of Jimmy's Sacrament residence and 850 miles north of El Centro, ran its front page headline:

TRUCKER SAID CHEATING ON FREEWAY JOB

The story said:

> *"James Fratianno, once described by the police as the 'West Coast Mafia Executioner,' was held today on $55,000 bail on an Imperial County warrant charging him with criminal conspiracy. Fratianno, 53, a trucking executive, was taken into custody Wednesday as he was boarding a flight to El Centro.*
>
> *A warrant charging Fratianno and four other people with felony conspiracy to defraud truckers working on two $5 million sections of Interstate 8 in Imperial County was issued Tuesday.*
>
> *Fred ReCupido, Kenneth Bentley, Nick Diacogianis, and Frank Bompensiero were arrested earlier.*
>
> *Imperial County District Attorney James E. Hamilton said the charges involved an arrangement between Fratianno and ReCupido and their truck driver employees, who by alleged misrepresentation were forced to sign purchase contracts for the trucks they drove.*
>
> *'Drivers, as a result, were fraudulently deprived of their rightful earned minimum wages, or were not paid for hours worked,' Hamilton said.*
>
> *Hamilton also said that more than 50 complaining witnesses had caused the state-federal investigation*

that could result in further charges in other jurisdictions."

Then, California state Attorney General, Thomas E. Lynch, got into the act.

The headline in the *San Bernardino County Sun* read:

LYNCH DETAILS CASE AGAINST UNION BUSTING FIRM

Lynch told the *Sun*:

"The union members were not only paid below union scale, but they were paid below the prevailing wage scale set by the Division of Highways as an agent for the Federal government.

Payroll deductions were paid for alleged payments on the trucks, insurance policies, fuel, repairs and parts and rentals of the trailers for the trucks.

This, in turn, led to Mafia loan sharks preying on the underpaid union members."

This is when the rats in Jimmy's inner circle began to crawl from their sewers. During the preliminary hearing into the case, in which sixty-six witnesses testified in a three month period, Fred ReCupido and Jimmy's crack mechanic, Kenneth Bentley, both decided to change sides and testify for the government. And in a surprise move, Superior Court Judge Victor Gillespie ordered the charges be dropped against Frank Bompensiero due to "lack of evidence."

Bomp's dismissal from the case turned out to be the biggest setback for Jimmy Fratianno, more than the charges filed against him. It seemed that Bomp abhorred the idea of going back to jail, and when push came to shove, FBI Agent Jack Armstrong was able to get Bomp to turn canary. The sweet tune Bomp sang for the feds concerned the misadventures of his old pal, Jimmy Fratianno, not only detailing whatever misdeeds Jimmy had committed in the past, but especially what Jimmy planned to do in the future.

The government also decided to press conspiracy charges against Jimmy's wife, Jewel, who did the actual bookkeeping concerning the underpayment of union members. This was done ostensibly to get Jimmy to crack and spill the beans on his other mob associates. But by this time Jimmy and Jewel were on the outs, and Jimmy had already taken up residence with his new squeeze: a neurotic, yet beautiful and bubbly drunk named Jean Bodul.

On one of his first trips to El Centro, Jimmy decided to fly back and forth instead of making the eighteen-hour round-trip in his new Caddy.

Jean was sitting in the tiny waiting room at the El Centro airport when Jimmy spotted her. She appeared to be in her early thirties, with soft blond hair and a body that wouldn't quit. Jimmy, never the shy one, offered to carry her bag when she stood up after the announcement was made for passengers to board the airplane headed to Los Angeles.

"Thanks," she said. "My name is Jean Bodul."

"A lovely woman like you should never be allowed to carry her own bag," Jimmy said.

"Are you going to Los Angeles too?" she said.

"No, I live in Sacramento, but I travel to Los Angeles often on business," Jimmy said.

Jimmy told Jean he was in the trucking business, and Jean told Jimmy that she was divorced and had a ten-year-old girl who was living with her mother in San Pedro.

When they reached the boarding gate, Jimmy said. "Why don't you give me your phone number, and I'll give you a call the next time I'm in Los Angeles."

"Are you married?" Jean said.

"For the time being, but we're getting divorced," Jimmy said.

Jean thought for a second, and then she wrote her Los Angeles phone number on a small piece of paper and handed it to Jimmy.

Then, she made an about-face, sashayed across the tarmac and boarded her plane. Jimmy didn't take his eyes off her until she disappeared from sight.

Jimmy made it a point to come to Los Angeles to see Jean quite often. They visited the swankiest restaurants; places where Jimmy and his reputation were well known. Jimmy made sure before he and Jean entered any eatery, the staff had been notified in advance so that they would give Jimmy the red-carpet treatment as soon as they passed through the front door.

On one occasion, the fawning and flattery at the Villa Capri on the Sunset Strip was so over-the-top, soon after they were seated, Jean blurted out, "My God, who are you anyway? Ally Kahn or Rubirosa?"

"I'm nobody," Jimmy said. "I just know the owner, Patsy, for years."

"Try telling that to these jokers jumping around her like they have ants in their pants," Jean said. "I don't dare look in their direction. They'll probably trip and break a leg getting here."

Soon, Jimmy sprung for a swanky apartment on Normandie Avenue in San Pedro for him to share with Jean as their love nest.

"Now you're my girlfriend," Jimmy told Jean.

It was a statement not a request, and Jean knew it. Why she didn't know was that her life would change immensely in ways that were, up to this point, unimaginable.

The divorce for Jimmy and Jewel Fratianno was finalized in late 1967. But the indignity of being married to Jimmy Fratianno didn't end until a year later.

In June of 1968, both Jewel Switzer (after her divorce she went back to using her maiden name) and Jimmy Fratianno were found guilty in a San Diego courtroom of one count of conspiracy and 15 counts of filing false statements with the federal government. When Federal Judge Edward Schwartz pronounced his sentence, Jewel was given a slap on the wrist with a $4,000 fine, no jail time, and no probation. Jimmy thought he had been given a gift from heaven, when the judge fined him $10,000, no jail time and only three years' probation. Jimmy was jailed until he paid the $10,000. But Jewel forked over the four grand, and walked out of Jimmy Fratianno's life for good. She died of cancer in1980.

However, Jimmy felt even a measly $10,000 fine was too much for him to pay. In jail, he immediately took "the pauper's oath" claiming, because of his hefty attorney's fees, he was now totally broke. Jimmy testified under oath that his only worldly possessions were a cracked diamond ring and 1967 automobile, of which he owned $1600 in payments.

On September 4, Jimmy lost his car and his cracked diamond ring, but gained his freedom when he walked out of the San Diego lockup like he was floating on air.

But Imperial County District Attorney James Hamilton was not finished fighting. He appealed Jimmy's sentencing, and he won that appeal. Jimmy was set to be tried again on fraud and conspiracy charges, but this time in Los Angeles, where Jimmy knew he had favorable judges.

But before his trial date arrived, Jimmy's lawyer, James Cantillon, reached a plea bargaining agreement with District Attorney Hamilton and his top assistant, Richard Huffman, in which Jimmy would plead guilty to one count of petty theft, a felony in California. The sentencing guidelines were one to three years in prison. However, Cantillon told Jimmy that D.A. Hamilton would not object if Jimmy was given just probation.

This is where Jimmy's old enemy, a Los Angeles police captain, also named James Hamilton, got his revenge.

On January 10, 1969, Jimmy appeared with counsel in the courtroom of Judge George Dell. Attached to Jimmy's probation report were scathing accusations by Los Angeles Police Captain Hamilton, that made it impossible for Judge Dell to give Jimmy probation.

In this report, which Judge Dell read aloud in court, Captain Hamilton wrote, "In the summer of 1966, it was discovered that James Fratianno had a girlfriend in the San Pedro area by the name of Jean Bodul. Investigation revealed that Bodul was a prostitute working out of the Hollywood area, where she maintained another apartment for just that purpose. Fratianno made frequent trips to the San Pedro area and was seen on many occasions in the company of Bodul."

The report also included a *Los Angeles Times* article which stated that, "Fratianno was identified as 'The Chicago Mafia's West Coast Executioner,' and like the Mafia has done in Chicago, Fratianno and his associates have made strong making efforts to infiltrate the California unions."

Both Jimmy and Cantillon were so incensed they almost crapped in their pants.

After Judge Del finished reading aloud Jimmy's probation report, Cantillon jumped to his feet, and screamed, "I would like a ten minute recess!"

Cantillon and Jimmy confronted both District Attorney Hamilton and his assistant, Huffman, in the corridor outside the courtroom.

"What the fuck just happened?" Cantillon screamed. "I thought we had a deal."

"Sorry, Mr. Cantillon," Huffman said. "But we have orders from the state attorney general, Tom Lynch, not to say anything at sentencing. Lynch says whatever Judge Dell does is fine with him."

"But that was not the deal we made," Cantillon said. "You agreed that you would tell the judge that you recommended probation."

"That deal is dead," Huffman said. "Word had gotten back to Lynch that Fratianno is going around saying he's got the Attorney General in his hip pocket."

Jimmy knew he told only his closest associates of his deal with Imperial County Attorney General Hamilton. So, if what

Huffman is saying is true, there was a rat somewhere in Jimmy's organization. Jimmy never suspected that rat was Frank "Bomp" Bompensiero.

"This is bullshit," Jimmy told Huffman. "I ain't talked to no one about this case. Give me a name!"

"Sorry, that's all I can say about this matter," Huffman said.

Cantillon went back into court, and he told Judge Dell that he wanted to withdraw Jimmy's guilty plea. Judge Dell said it was too late for that, but that he would wait until August to pronounce sentencing. Jimmy was immediately released on bail, but he was not too happy.

On August 11, 1970, Jimmy again appeared before Judge Dell. As Judge Dell was ready to announce his decision, Cantillon stood up. Judge Dell shot Cantillon the evil eye.

"Do not interrupt me," Judge Dell told Cantillon. "After reading the probation report, I am now revoking probation for Mr. Fratianno. I have considered the entire matter, and I hereby sentence Mr. Fratianno to one-to-three years in prison."

Within hours, Jimmy "The Wesel" Fratianno was again a resident at San Quentin State Prison.

After four months in San Quentin, Jimmy was transferred to the Southern Reception Guidance Center (SRGC) in Chino, where he got the cushy job of supervising the maintenance crew. Weeks later, his attorney, James Cantillon, told Jimmy that he would have to serve the entire three years in prison, with no chance of parole. But Jimmy knew how to do good time: just concentrate on your daily duties, and forget there was an outside world. But with a girlfriend like Jean, that was difficult to do.

While he was stewing in SRGC, Jimmy found out through his mob cronies that Jean was going through an especially bad time. She was getting drunk almost daily and sometimes she wound up in bed with men whose names she could neither pronounce nor remember. With no one to support her with her extravagant lifestyle, Jean decided to hook up with someone with one foot in the grave and the other on a banana peel and was loaded with cash. His name was Zeppo Marx, the fourth of the famous Marx Brothers comedians. Marx, then 72-years-old, had just been divorced from his wife, Barbara, who in turn, had married Frank Sinatra.

Jean met Marx at the wedding of her friend, Bo Wheat, who married golfer Ken Venturi, the winner of the 1964 Open Golf Tournament. Frank Sinatra paid for his friend Venturi's wedding, and it was Sinatra himself who introduced Marx to Jean. Soon, they became a popular item in Hollywood and in Las Vegas.

After about six months of courtship, Marx insisted that Jean move in with him. Jean would not have minded if a marriage proposal had been included, but Marx was adamant.

"No, I can't think about marriage now. I've just been divorced," Marx told her. "But if you move in with me, maybe later that's something I would consider."

Jean didn't like the idea one bit.

"If you don't marry me, I'm not moving in with you," she told Marx.

One night in April of 1973, the couple got into a heated argument at the Tamarisk Country Club in Rancho Mirage. Jean tried to leave the country club, but Marx would have none of that. Marx chased Jean down the driveway of the country club, and as Jean tried to get into her car, Marx attacked her, pulling her hair and banging her head against her car door.

Crying, she went back to Jimmy at SRGC and told him what had happened. If Jimmy had been on the outside world, he would have handled the Marx situation himself. But he didn't need to get involved with something that could jeopardize his release after serving the full three years in prison. So, he told Jean to let it lay until he was a free man, and then he'd decided what to do about Zeppo Marx.

In 1979, after she was married to Jimmy and in the Witness Protection Program with him, Jimmy persuaded Jean to sue Marx for every buck he had. The truth is at this point Jimmy needed the cash.

Jean filed suit in state court in Idaho, California, asking for $350,000 in damages.

On the witness stand, Jean came off as a ditzy broad, extremely good looking, but not very bright. On the other hand, Marx, although cultured, appeared haughty and out of touch with the needs of the common person. The jury deliberated only an hour and a half, and they came back with a verdict in favor of Jean, but only to the tune of $20,690.

After her lawyer took his cut, Jean cleared less that fifteen grand. Jimmy was pissed.

"Shit, I used used to make more than that holding up cards games in the 1930s, Jimmy told Jean.

On August 28, 1973, Jimmy the Weasel" Fratianno strolled out of SRGC in Chino, and into a waiting limousine, which was hired by his best friend in the mob, Johnny Roselli. In the back seat was Jean. With money Jimmy had sent her through a friend, Jean had rented an apartment in a suburb of Los Angeles, and they settled in just like old times.

Two weeks later, Jimmy was on a flight to Miami to see Roselli, who, after serving four years in prison, was now living in Plantation, twenty miles north of Miami, with his sister and brother-in-law, Edith and Joseph Daigle. Roselli considered himself retired from the mob, but his pals in Chicago felt differently.

It seemed that a lot had transpired in the Chicago Outfit since Jimmy went away in 1970 and none of it was any good.

After Jimmy and Roselli had dinner at Tony Roma's in North Miami, the two old cronies sat at the bar and reminisced about their good old days, which Roselli felt had turned to crap.

Both men ordered Remy Martin. Jimmy took a sip of his drink, then he grabbed Roselli's right forearm to get his attention.

"Listen to this. When I first got out a few weeks ago, I get a phone call from Johnny Regace," Jimmy said. "He's now calling himself Dominick Brooklier. What is he now, a fucking Englishman?"

"Yeah, I hear he's now the underboss in Los Angeles under Nick Licata, who took over when Nick DeSimone died," Roselli said. "And here's the kicker – his real name is not even Regace. It's Brucculeri Domenico. I guess he gets the Brooklier from his real first name."

"Well, I also hear that Nick Licata ain't doing so good health-wise," Jimmy said. "That means if he kicks off, Regace, or Brooklier, or whatever the fuck he calls himself at the time, will be the new boss in Los Angeles."

"Well, the way I hear it, the L.A family is in the shit again," Roselli said. "You and Bomp were the only real gangsters in the whole crew. The rest are old men because nobody got made in the past 20 years in L.A."

"Yeah, you're right about that," Jimmy says. "There's no new blood to carry on the tradition."

"So what did Brooklier want?" Roselli said.

"I was just getting to that, "Jimmy said. "Brooklier asks me to meet with him at a restaurant on Sunset Plaza Drive. I get there first, and then he strolls in with Pete Milano. He tells me that not only is Pete now a made guy, but that's he's a capo. I look at the piece of shit Milano and I wanted to laugh in their faces. Milano's a nobody; never did a piece of work in his life. If someone should have been made capo, it was Bomp."

"I hear Bomp's on the outs with that crew," Roselli said. "They say he talks too much."

"Bomp always talked too much, but he's got more balls than all those guys put together," Jimmy said.

Jimmy took another sip of Remy.

"So Brooklier tells me he just got finished talking with the old man, Licata, and they want to know, since I'm with Chicago now, what I'm doing in town," Jimmy said. "He says they've been doing some inquiring about me, and they don't like what they're hearing. They hear I'm trying to open up my own book in California; which I am, but fuck them anyway.

"So now I tear into him. I tell him I saved his life when I talked him into walking away from Mickey Cohen. He tells me, 'What are you getting so mad about? I'm just passing on what Nick told me.' I tell him 'What the fuck do I care about Nick Licata?' He tells me, 'You know the rules. You've got to check in with us before handing any action in our country.' Imagine the nerve of those cocksuckers."

"Don't worry, Jimmy," Roselli said. "Louie Dragna is with that crew, and he's just as bad as the rest of them. But the way I hear it, and this is only from what I read in the newspapers, the whole bunch of them are in trouble with the law. When they go down, you can step right in and take over. I know Chicago will back you up on this one."

Sure enough, in March of 1974, Pete Milano and six men under him were convicted of running a floating illegal gambling venture in San Fernando Valley (floating means they moved the game from night to night to different places). To make matters worse, Milano was using loaded dice, marked cards, and crooked roulette wheels, to fleece the legitimate people who frequented the games.

John Ludlow DuBeck was an ex-con who, along with his wife Frances, helped Milano's crew rig the gambling operation. When he got pinched, DuBeck was facing big-time in the slammer. So he agreed to cooperate and testify in court and Milano and his crew. But one week before the trial started, both DuBeck and his wife were riddled with bullets outside their Las Vegas apartment building. This broke the long-standing mob rules that prohibited murder in the state of Nevada.

Even with the two key witnesses eliminated, Milano was convicted and sentenced to four years in prison. No one was ever arrested for the murders of John and Frances DuBeck.

In July 1974, a federal grand jury indicted Brooklier, Milano and ten others on charges of racketeering, conspiracy and extortion against bookmakers, loan sharks, and pornographers in the Los Angeles area. In October, Nick Licata died, and Brooklier, even though he was indicted and was facing jail time, was anointed the new mob boss in California. Brooklier immediately named Sam Sciortino, originally from Chicago, as his underboss.

As bad as things were In California, they were just as bad for the Outfit in Chicago; especially Sam Giancana who had been instrumental in bringing both Roselli and Fratianno into the Chicago Outfit.

In 1966, Giancana did a year in jail for refusing to testify at a grand jury hearing. Feeling Giancana was attracting too much federal scrutiny, Paul Ricca and Tony Accardo removed Giancana as the day-to-day boss of the Chicago Outfit and replaced him with Joseph "Joey Doves" Aiuppa.

After he was released from prison, Giancana was disenchanted by the way he was treated by his so-called pals in Chicago, and he relocated to Mexico, where he had contacts in gambling, drug, and the pornographic movie industry. Giancana also had organized crime associates as far away as Iran, where he established a foothold in the gambling business. Giancana was raking in so much cash, he was able to live in a lavish mansion in Cuernavaca and was still was able to pay the local Mexican politicians and law enforcement personal a tidy sum in graft money each month.

Tony Accardo was not happy that Giancana was making so much money in Mexico and Iran and not kicking it back to his pals in Chicago. Accardo demanded a share of Giancana's Mexican and Iranian profits, but Giancana flatly refused, saying, "This money I made all by myself out of the country. It has nothing to do with Chicago."

Accardo sent an emissary to Mexico, and he told him to explain to Giancana "The facts of life. And I do mean *life*."

Giancana knew, with his contacts in Mexico, he was untouchable by the Chicago Outfit. So he told Accardo's messenger boy to tell "Joe Batters" a.k.a. "Tony the Tuna" to "go stick his baseball bat up his ass."

This was all well and good for Giancana. But in the fall of 1974, after a change in the Mexican political hierarchy, the Mexican militia dragged Giancana out of bed in the middle of the night. They put Giancana on a plane, and when he arrived at Chicago's O'Hare Airport, he was wearing house slippers and carrying his bathrobe.

The word was out; Giancana was back in Chicago, and he wanted to regain his power. This is when Johnny Roselli got very nervous. A month after Giancana resurfaced in Chicago, Roselli phoned Jimmy at his home.

"Joe Batters is now in power," Roselli said. "But he leaves the daily hassles of being boss to Joe Aiuppa. Jackie Cerrone is the underboss, and Batters acts as consigliere."

"Where does that leave us?" Jimmy said. "I hardly know all three. Sam was our guy in Chicago."

"It leaves us fucked, that where it leaves us," Roselli said. "My situation with Batters is piss poor. There's jealousy that goes all the way back to Capone's days, and there's nothing I can do about it. This guy's got me on his shit list.

"I'm giving it straight to you, Jimmy. There's nothing you can do when the bosses turn on you. That's the trouble with this thing of ours. We're sitting ducks. You, me and Sam Giancana."

"Yeah, well I got a good little bookie operation going in San Francisco, and Bomp is the main guy in San Diego," Jimmy said. "Nobody's tough enough to touch us over here on the West Coast. I think I'll make my moves here."

"Good idea, Jimmy," Roselli said. "Those guys in Los Angeles will take you back in a second. As for me, I told the boys in Chicago that I'm retired. I don't need the money, and I don't need the aggravation. I'm staying here in Miami, and that's it.

That's when Jimmy Fratianno got the idea that getting in bed with the feds wasn't such a bad idea after all. He contacted special Agent Lowell "Larry" Lawrence, who had tried to turn Jimmy several times while he was in Chino.

Jimmy met Lawrence once or twice a month, always in West Coast hotel rooms. Jimmy gave Lawrence information on who was doing what in California, in Chicago and in Cleveland, and Lawrence paid Jimmy generously with government money for that information. To Jimmy it was a win-win situation. The government gave Jimmy cold hard cash, and Jimmy gave them tiny tidbits on the underworld that any mob dope on the street knew about.

As far as Jimmy was concerned, his mob allegiances in Chicago were out and California was back in. He figured it was just a matter of time before he took over everything on the West Coast.

In February of 1975, Jimmy got the break he was waiting for. Louie Dragna, a blast from the past, contacted Jimmy in San Francisco and told him to take a flight to Ontario, California, a mid-sized town 35 miles east of downtown Los Angeles. Since his release from prison, Jimmy had run into Dragna once or twice, but Jimmy never considered Dragna a friend, let alone a close buddy. Yet, Dragna told Jimmie it was extremely important that they meet right away.

Dragna met Jimmy at the airport, and they two men absconded to a local mob run restaurant. While they were sipping pre-meal cocktails, Dragna got right to the point.

"I'm sure you know Brooklier and Sciortino are going to prison in a few months," Dragna said.

"Yeah, I've read about it, and it looks like they've made pretty good deals for themselves," Jimmy said. "Those guys were looking at ten years. What did they get, two years?"

"Brooklier got 20 months, and Sciortino got 18 months," Dragna said.

The waiter placed steak dinners on the table in front of both men.

After taking a couple of bites of his steak, Dragna put down his fork and knife, and said, "Those guys have asked me to take over the family while they're away. I told them I would do it only if you came in with me. You know, we'll run the family together. They liked the idea. Are you interested?"

Jimmy wanted to lean across the table and kiss Louie Dragna full on the lips.

It made sense that Louie Dragna, who was making millions legitimately in the clothing business - the Roberta Manufacturing Company - didn't want to get his hands dirty with the day-to-day headaches of running an organized crime enterprise.

"I might be interested, but how would this work?" Jimmy said.

"We'll both be acting bosses," Dragna said. "But you'll be carrying most of the load. I'm so busy with Roberta, I don't know which day of the week it is."

"Well, let's say I agree to the proposition," Jimmy said. "I still got to get permission from Chicago."

"That's no problem," Dragna said. "Just tell Joe Batters, or whomever is running the show in Chicago, we're going to be acting bosses while Brooklier and Sciortino are in jail. That's less than two years. They can get in touch with me to confirm the deal."

"Okay, let's say we can arrange that," Jimmy said. "There's no way I'm relocating to Los Angeles. I'm doing real well in San Francisco, and I'm not coming down to Los Angeles to make money for a bunch of deadheads. I'll set things up, start making some moves. But the guys in Los Angeles are going to do all the work. Not me."

"That's fine with me," Dragna said. "You do what you have to do, and I'll back you up one hundred percent."

Jimmy couldn't believe his good fortune. He was dead in his bed in Chicago; in danger of getting whacked because of his closeness to Sam Giancana. And now he was going to run the West Coast mob, if only for a little less than two years. Jimmy was certain if he did a good job, he would again be promoted back to captain in California after Brooklier and Sciortino did their time.

Plus, there was the steady cash coming in regularly from the feds. It was only pocket money, but the idea of him milking the government and giving them useless information to boot, gave Jimmy a boner.

Finally, at 61 years of age, and after three stints in the can, Jimmy Fratianno would be boss, albeit an acting boss, who would demand respect from all over the country, including New York City.

The boner killer who burst the bubble of Jimmy's euphoria was his increasingly-erratic girlfriend, Jean Bodul.

Jean and her daughter, Annette, had left their digs in Murrieta Springs, which is 90 miles south of Los Angeles and a seven-hour trip from San Francisco, and moved in with Jimmy in his two-bedroom San Francisco apartment. Annette had told Jimmy that her mother's drinking had gotten out of control and that she could no longer handle her alone. Jimmy's first impulse was to say no to the move, but after much prodding from Annette, whom Jimmy was dearly fond of, he finally agreed.

Jean and Annette were barely in San Francisco a month, when Jimmy came home and found Annette hysterical.

"My mother got drunk again, and we had an argument," Annette told Jimmy. "She ran out of the apartment in her bare feet, and I'm afraid she's going to kill herself."

Jimmy jumped in his car and began driving all around the neighborhood streets and side-streets, figuring Jean couldn't have gotten far barefooted. It took Jimmy more than three hours, but he finally found Jean on a deserted side street, disheveled and walking a around in circles like a lunatic. He tried to reason with her, but she just ran away from him.

But, before Jean could make it too the corner, she fainted. When she hit the pavement, she rolled over onto her back. Jimmy bent down to pick her up, and he noticed vomit all over the bottom of her dress. He picked her up, deposited her into the back seat of his car and drove her back to his apartment.

The following day, Jimmy stood home with Jean and Annette until Jean woke up at around two in the afternoon. The first thing she did was light up a cigarette, then between spluttering coughs and chokes, she told Jimmy, "I've made two decisions today. The first is that I'm joining A.A. I've given this a lot of thought, and I know I can't do it myself. I need professional help."

Jimmy, not being the brightest of bulbs on the subject, said, "Are you crazy! You're not an alcoholic. You don't even drink every day. Alcoholic are drunk from morning to night. And they drink every day."

"I'm sorry, Jimmy," she said. "I need help and that's all there is to it."

Jimmy agreed that maybe she did need assistance with handling alcohol, so he agreed he would take her to Alcoholic Anonymous meetings.

"I'll even go inside with you to see what the fuss is all about," Jimmy said. "Now what's the second decision?"

As so as the words left his lips, Jimmy knew the answer.

"My second decision is that we're getting married, or it's all over between us," she said. "I know I've said that before, and you ignored me. But this time I'm serious. So you better make up your mind."

Jimmy let her remarks roll around in his brain for a minute, then he thought, "Why the fuck not?"

"Okay, I'll make a deal with you," Jimmy said. "You go to these meetings every day for a month. If you're still sober after that, we'll get married."

Jimmy Fratianno, for once in his life, kept his word. Six weeks later, he took Jean to Reno for a quickie marriage. They stood overnight, and when they returned to San Francisco, Jimmy rented them a three-bedroom cottage at the tiny town of Moss Beach, 35 miles southeast of San Francisco and right on the Pacific Ocean. This location was especially appealing to Jimmy, since it was a little more than a mile away from the Half Moon Airport.

With Jean and Annette settled in Moss Beach, Jimmy hopped on a plan and headed for Cleveland. He planned to meet with old pals, Tony "Tony Dope" Delsanter and Leo Moceri, who was now the underboss of Cleveland's Mayfield Road mob. The reason for the trip was because Jimmy wanted to run past his old friends Louie Dragna's proposal for them to take over the West Coast mob until Brooklier and Sciortino got out of the can.

When Jimmy's plane arrived in Cleveland, Tony Dope was there to pick him up at the airport. Tony Dope brought Jimmy to a high class mob-owned Italian restaurant in Cleveland Little Italy called Sabbatino's. Leo Moceri had a piece of the place, and he was waiting for them at a private dining room in the back.

After dining on a fine meal of veal parmesan and stuffed shells, and gulping down the best Chianti in the joint, Jimmy told them about Louie Dragna's proposal.

"They don't know I came here to run it past you first," Jimmy said. "So, what do you think?"

"You've been around for a long time," Moceri said. "I think you should take it. After those two cafones get out of jail, then we'll see where you stand."

"I agree," Tony Dope said. "What have you got to lose? Those two mooks are useless. The might even decide to give you the job full time when they get out. The might not want the aggravation any more. "

"I see what you're saying, "Jimmy said. "But these are the same people who stole all my money when I was in the can."

"Yeah, but they're all going to jail," Moceri said. "You'll be in charge. You can do things any way you see fit."

"That's right, Jimmy," Tony Dope said. "With them all gone, it's a whole new deal. Revamp the family. Put everything in order so you impress the mob bosses all over the country. Then when they get out, we'll put it to a vote with the boys in New York. You have our backing here in Cleveland, and a lot can happen in twenty months."

Jimmy's went straight from Cleveland to Chicago to meet with the Outfit's boss, Joey Aiuppa and his underboss Jackie Cerone. Both Chicago gangsters were oblivious to the happenings on the West Coast, and after all, Jimmy was still technically with the Chicago Outfit. Jimmy hoped that the Sam Giancana situation did not yet put him on the Chicago Outfit's hit list, and he knew he was taking a big chance by going to Chicago alone. But after his positive meeting in Cleveland with Tony Dope and Moceri, Jimmy was confident of the outcome. Besides, Leo Moceri had told Jimmy he would call ahead to Chicago and put in a good work for him.

After filling in Aiuppa and Cerone on the details of his meeting with Louie Dragna, Jimmy said, "I told them I had to get your blessing on my transfer back to the West Coast."

Aiuppa thought it over for a few seconds, then he nodded towards Cerone, who nodded back.

"Ok, Jimmy, you can tell them you have our blessings." Aiuppa said. "Normally I wouldn't agree, but they making you acting boss changes everything. But remember your friends here in Chicago when they need you. Capice?"

Jimmy took the next plane back to the Half Moon Airport. He was glad he had accomplished getting the blessings of both the Cleveland and the Chicago mobs. But he still had the problem concerning his past cooperation with the FBI. Larry Lawrence had given Jimmy close to twenty grand in the past two years, and Jimmy had given Lawrence mostly bupkis. But the feds would surely know, from other informants, that Jimmy was now in charge in California.

After much thought, Jimmy decided he'd put off deciding what to do about the FBI until he had a clearer head. Right now he was drunk with the power of being a legitimate mob boss. He could deal with the FBI later.

Days before Tony Brooklier was set to report to prison, he summoned Jimmy to his office, which was buried in the back of the Los Angeles Clothing Mart, owned by Vic Werber, a legitimate guy who liked hanging around with wiseguys. For the privilege of their company, Brooklier was shaking down Werber for tens of thousands in protection money. If Werber didn't pay what Brooklier demanded, Werber was made to understand that maybe the Los Angeles Clothing Mart would go up in flames with Werber tied to chair inside.

When Jimmy arrived, in the room with Brooklier were Louie Dragna, Sam Sciortino, and Pete Milano. Werber was present too, but he wisely vacated the premises before he heard things that might be hazardous to his health.

Brooklier greeted Jimmy like Jimmy was a long lost friend. But Jimmy knew differently.

"Jimmy, it's good we're back together again," Brooklier said, squeezing Jimmy's right hand. "This should have happened a long time ago."

"I got the blessing from the old man in Chicago," Jimmy said. "I'll do the best I can for you while you're away. I'll pull a few moves and make us all some money."

That sounded great to Brooklier, and he gave Jimmy a tip on a shakedown that was sure to make money for everyone concerned.

"See Jimmy, there's this guy here named Ruben Sturman," Brooklier said. "He's got about 50 porno shop just here in town. He lives in a fucking mansion in Shaker Heights. But he ain't kicking back to us."

"I know the guy," Jimmy said. "His protection is Tony Zappi in New York City. Tony's with the Gambino family; the biggest family in New York."

"Well, a few years back, Sturman was operating in Cleveland," Brooklier said. "So we sent someone there to smack him around a bit. Of course, the Cleveland mob was in on the deal too. Just as we figured, Sturman runs to Zappi in New York City. We called Zappi in advance and told him about the deal. Zappi hits Sturman for two hundred grand, and we all whacked it up. Now Sturman is in our town raking in the dough.

"Why don't you get Tony Dope or Leo to get someone to come down here and shake up Sturman again. He'll run to Zappi, and we'll all make a bundle again. This time we should shoot for half a million. The guy's fucking loaded."

"Yeah, I'll talk with my guys in Cleveland," Jimmy said. "But Zappi is out of the picture now. He got into trouble, and he's lamming it from the law. The guys in charge of all the porno in New York are Mickey Zaffarano, who's with Carmine Galante's crew, and another guy called Debe (Robert DiBernardo) a made guy with the Gambinos."

"That's fine," Brooklier said. "You can handle it. These guys are all friends of ours. Besides, Sturman ain't the only porno guy in town that needs straightening out. There's Willie Bittner, Jack Molinas, Mike Pinkus, and Teddy Gaswirth. They're all selling smut and making a mint in California, and we ain't seeing a cent."

"Okay, I'll see what I can do while you're away," Jimmy said.

The five men exited Werber's office, and as they strolled to the parking lot, "Brooklier whispered to Jimmy, "What's the situation with you and Bomp?"

"We're good friends," Jimmy said.

"Well, while we're gone, I need you to straighten out this guy," Brooklier said. "He's got no respect for anyone in our family."

Jimmy knew "straighten out" usually meant "whack out" in mob parlance. But until he was given an explicit order, Jimmy decided to stay far away from Frank "Bomp" Bompensiero, lest he got caught in the crossfire.

On March 9, 1975, the headline in the New York Times said,

Aides Say Robert F. Kennedy Told of Plot to Assassinate Castro.

The article led with:

> *"Two former aids to the late Robert F. Kennedy said that he told them in 1967 that agents of the Central Intelligence agency had contracted with the Mafia in an aborted plot to assassinate Premier Fidel Castro before the Bay of Pigs Invasion of 1961."*

The article went on to name the Mafia members involved in the plot to kill Castro as Sam Giancana and Johnny Roselli.

This article compelled the government to form a Senate Select Committee on Intelligence Activities with the expressed purpose of investigating whether there was, in fact, a CIA plot to kill Castro. Two men who were on the top of Senate Committee's list of people to interview was Sam Giancana and Jimmy Roselli. And as if the Chicago Outfit needed another reason to whack both men, they got their wish when both agreed to testify before a government committee, which is a definite no-no in the world of organized crime. This offense was in addition to the fact that Giancana and Roselli, in the early 1960s, should never have spoken to the CIA in the first place. Speaking to law enforcement merits the death penalty in the mob.

After Roselli had already testified before the committee and told them nothing that wasn't public record already, Giancana was up to bat next. But two days before his scheduled court date, someone shot Giancana once in the back of his head in the basement of his Oak Park, Illinois home. And after his body had been turned over, six more bullets were fired into Giancana's head, face, and chest. It was obvious Giancana's knew his killer because he willingly let his killer into his house. Giancana's home was supposed to be under police protection until he testified in court, but someone had mysteriously dismissed the police guard in front of Giancana's house minutes before his murder.

After hearing about his old friend's slaying, Roselli immediately fled Miami. He took a plane to Los Angeles, and minutes after his arrival, Roselli phoned Jimmy and asked for an emergency meeting to discuss both their futures. Jimmy figured the safest place for such a meeting would be in the Los Angeles law offices of his lawyer, James Cantillon.

Jimmy and Roselli huddled in Cantillon's law library, without Cantillon being present. Cantillon figured the less he knew about the situation the better it would be for his health.

As he paced back and forth in the law office like a man on death row waiting for the signal to sit in the electric chair, Roselli looked as white as a sheet.

"They killed a dead man, Jimmy," Roselli said. "He could barely climb a flight of stairs. Sam was just in Houston last week with Dr. Debakey because he had a blood clot in his chest."

Roselli slammed his hand down on the law library desk.

"It's was that motherfucking Aiuppa and that cocksucker Joe Batters," Roselli said. "They're using the excuse that Sam wanted to get back into power in Chicago, but that's bullshit. Sam was finished with that, just like me."

"Johnny, you're not on safe ground here," Jimmy said. "The way I heard it, Sam's murder was a commission contract. The boys in New York already okayed it. I also heard you might be next on their list. Remember, they told all of us when we got made that we go into this thing of ours alive and leave it dead."

"Fuck them, I'm going back to Miami," Roselli said. "They know where to find me if they want to do something. But I tell you this, I ain't going easily."

After heartfelt goodbyes, Jimmy dropped off Roselli in San Pedro, and then he drove to a liquor store parking lot in the same town for a meeting with his co-boss, Louie Dragna. He parked his car next to Dragna's and jumped into the passenger seat next to him.

Dragna cut right to the chase.

"I talked to the old man (Brooklier) and he told me he already spoke to you about Bomp," Dragna said. "What are you doing in this respect?"

"Well, I've been busy lately, and I haven't been able to discuss the situation with Bomp," Jimmy said.

"Well, there's nothing to discuss, Jimmy," Dragna said. "The old man wants Bomp clipped. I know you consider Bomp a friend, but he's not. Bomp's been bad-rapping you all over the country. And not just you. He's talking about the old man, Pete Milano, and even your friend Johnny Roselli. And we've gotten word that he's talking to the feds too."

Jimmy almost blew a heart valve. His face got hot and his chest began pounding like a bass drum. Now he realized why he had been brought back into the fold. Nobody else was capable of killing Bomp. Bomp had whacked many men, and he knew all the setups. Bomp would see jerks like Dragna, Brooklier, and Sciortino coming from a mile away. And since the order had come from up top, Jimmy couldn't refuse otherwise he'd get clipped himself.

"You scheming motherfucker! You always make a guy a rat when you want to clip them," Jimmy said. "Okay, I'll do what the old man says, but this is the last time I do this type of shit for you guys."

Dragna put his arm on Jimmy's shoulder. Jimmy wanted to slap it off, but then thought better.

"Look Jimmy, we don't expect you do to the hit yourself," Dragna said. "We know Bomp's your good friend. He trusts you. We just need you to set it up, and let someone else do the hit."

"Who the fuck in your crew is capable of killing a guy like Bomp?" Jimmy said. "Bomp will see it coming and clip the guy you sent to clip him."

"We got several capable guys," Dragna said. "There's Sal Pinelli, Tony's son, Jack LoCicero, who goes all the way back to my uncle Jack's days, and Mike Rizzi (Rizzitello). You and Rizzi are close, and you always said he was a good man. Take your pick, but the old man is pretty anxious about this. So give it your top priority."

Jimmy decided to change the subject.

"I put that Sturman plan into motion," Jimmy said. "My guys in Cleveland roughed him up already. We should be hearing from New York any day now."

"Great," Dragna said. "The old man wants to see you. He's in the prison hospital in Terminal Island."

"What happened?" Jimmy said. "He was fine when I saw him a couple of weeks ago."

"He's got heart trouble," Dragna said. "He had a slight heart attack. He's not feeling so good right now."

Jimmy made the required trip to see Brooklier, and the old man repeated what Louie Dragna had already told Jimmy. Bomp had to go, and it was Jimmy job to make sure Bomp went. Jimmy assured the old man that he was right on top of the situation.

"Listen, Louie had a great idea to start the setup," Brooklier said. "I'm going to make Bomp my consigliere. This way he'll never figure we're looking to clip him. What do you think?"

Jimmy told his boss he thought that was a great idea. And as he left the prison hospital, Jimmy thought it peculiar that Brooklier looked so chipper and upbeat for a man with a bad heart.

Jimmy figured that Brooklier had heart trouble alright, but that was because he lacked one to begin with.

In the fall of 1976, things began to look rosier for Jimmy Fratianno when he was introduced to "Fat Tommy" Marson, a bowling ball-sized thug with a 50-inch waist and a permanent glow of booze in his blood-shot eyes.

Marson, a convicted bank robber, burglar, and con man extraordinaire, had gone reasonably straight for years and was an almost-legitimate millionaire living in a million dollar home on the 16th fairway of a golf course in Rancho Mirage, an exclusive resort city in the Palm Springs area. The ultra-exclusive Rancho Mirage was called the "Playground of Presidents." Among its residents were President Gerald Ford, and disgraced Vice President Spiro Agnew. President Ronald Reagan vacationed in Rancho Mirage, as did Richard Nixon, who was impeached and forced to resign in the Watergate scandal. Philanthropist Walter Annenberg owned an estate called "Sunnylands" at Rancho Mirage and on any given day, stars like Fred Astaire, Ginger Rodger, Mary Martin, Bob Hope, Bing Crosby, and even Queen Elizabeth II could be seen cavorting on the grounds of "Sunnylands."

However, what impressed Jimmy most about Marson was that he was a frequent house guest, and vice versa, of Frank Sinatra, who lived less than a half a mile away from Marson in Rancho Mirage on a street aptly named "Frank Sinatra Drive."

To insure his privacy, Sinatra had put a sign on the locked gate in front of his house that said: "You better have a damn good reason for ringing this damn bell."

What Jimmy didn't know about Marson was that the FBI was keeping a close watch on him, and had, in fact, received permission from a judge to wiretap Marson's phone.

It was mobster and degenerate killer, Irving "Slick" Shapiro, from Detroit's "Purple Gang," who, at Marson's request, took Jimmy to see Marson at his home. Shapiro had stiffed Jimmy for $20,000 in the 1950's, and he was one of the few men whom Jimmy would let get away with such an affront.

Marson had invested $400,000 in the building of the Westchester Premier Theater in Tarrytown, New York, which was just a 45 minute drive from the bright lights of Manhattan. Members of the Genovese, Columbo, and Gambino crime family were heavily involved in Westchester Premier Theater project, and the deal was so good, Carlo Gambino invested a few hundred grand of his own cash in the venture. Gambino's cousin, Big Paul Castellano, who would become boss when Gambino passed away in October of 1976, invested a reputed $100,000.

But mobsters like Greg DePalma, Richie "Nerves" Fusco and Louie "Dome" Pacella (a personal pal of Sinatra's) never had any intention of running a legitimate business. Because they paid so much money for famous acts like Sinatra, Dean Martin and Diana Ross (they paid Ross $235,000 for five days' work, more than she earned for similar work in Las Vegas), it was impossible to run the business in the black unless a lot of skimming was involved.

The gangsters skimmed from the concession stands, and they skimmed from the souvenir stands. The mobsters even installed 300-400 movable seats near the stage, and the ticket sales from those seats ($100-and-up per seat) went directly into the mobster's pockets without the IRS being any the wiser.

On paper, a stockbroker named Eliot Weisman was the owner of the Westchester Premier Theater. But he had as much say in the operation as did a minority stockholder in George Steinbrenner's New York Yankees. Soon, the Westchester Premier Theater was so far in the red, it ran the risk of closing and stiffing the legitimate stockholders, like entertainers Alan King, Steve Lawrence and Edie Gorme, all of whom had no idea of the thievery going on behind the scenes.

The problem Marson had being involved in the Westchester Premier Theater was that he had no muscle to back his play. He couldn't go up against mobsters like DePalma, Fusco, Pacella, and especially Carlo Gambino, without running the risk of getting whacked. Marson needed someone big in the mob to be his rabbi, and since Jimmy Fratianno had just been anointed acting-boss of the California mob and was known to be a stone killer, he was the perfect person to represent Marson's interests in New York.

Jimmy and Slick Shapiro were sipping pina coladas by Marson's pool, when the "Fat Man" made his appearance, carrying a Bloody Mary in a glass the size of his head. Shapiro made the introductions, and Marson got right to the point. Marson told Jimmy what and who and how much was involved, and why he was in danger of losing his entire investment in the Westchester Premier Theater.

"Looks like you fell in a snake pit," Jimmy told Marson. "What do you need from me?"

"Well, I'd like to get my money back, but not right away," Marson said. "What I want now is a bigger piece of the skim. These guys are holding back and giving me bupkis."

"What's in it for me?" Jimmy said.

"Well, if you can get me a bigger piece of the skim, I'll give you half the difference," Marson said. "Then, when I bail out and get my $400,000, I'll invest it here in California, in real estate, or whatever, and you'll get half the profits here too."

"Okay, make the arrangements for me to go to New York, and I'll see what I can do," Jimmy said. "I don't know these guys personally, but except for Carlo Gambino, none of them can go up against me."

"There's two more things I think I should mention," Marson said "Nino Gaggi is also involved. He's a captain in the Gambinos, and he invested two hundred grand. Plus, this Louie Dome, Sinatra's pal, is with Funzi Tieri – the boss of the Genovese family."

"Well, that's okay with me," Jimmy said. "I'm the acting boss here in California, so at a sitdown, as long as I don't get out of line, I carry as much weight as any of them."

In early March, Jimmy and Marson flew first class (at Marson's expense) on TWA to New York City. The reason for the trip was ostensibly to attend a $500 a plate for Frank Sinatra, who was being honored as Entertainer of the Year by the Friars Club. The Westchester Premier Theater had bought a table for ten for the dinner, and Jimmy and Marson were set to occupy two of those seats, alongside the major players who Jimmy needed to meet if he was going to properly represent Marson's interests.

Jimmy and Marson checked into the Tarrytown's Ramada Inn, and a few hours later, Greg DePalma arrived with his wife, Bobbi (who had a $500 a week no-show job at the theater), and Richie Fusco to drive them into the city for the Friars Club dinner. At their table, Jimmy met Eliot Weisman and his mother Ruth Rosenberg, who had invested $75,000 in the Westchester Premier Theater, the only cash investment anyone in the Weisman clan had in the doomed venture.

Everyone had a grand old time at the Friars Club Dinner. Hoard Cosell emceed the show along with Johnny Carson's sidekick,

Ed McMahon. Governor Hugh Carey was there to honor Sinatra, and so was the mayor of New York City, Abraham Beame. Even disgraced former Vice President Spiro Agnew made an appearance, and Agnew being at this event justified what Jimmy thought this dinner to be - just another scam to make money for the mob. Jimmy wondered who skimmed how much of the more than $250,000 shelled out that night by more than 500 Friar Club guests.

After the show, Jimmy and Marson visited DePalma's Westchester palatial home, where Jimmy agreed to attend Sinatra's concert at the Westchester Premier Theater in April.

The fun was just starting.

A few weeks later Jimmy flew back to New York, and he stood at the Rye Hilton. Although he spent most afternoons surveying the situation at the Westchester Premier Theater, Jimmy's main objective was to circulate around known mob hangouts at night to meet as many "amico nostras" as he could. With the Westchester Premier Theater wiseguys, DePalma, Fusco, and Pacella doing the initial introductions, Jimmy met such notables at "Louie Beans" Fucceri of the Bonanno crime family, Andrew Russo, a capo in the Colombo crime family, and Jimmy "Nap" Napoli who was under Tony Salerno of the Genovese crime family.

Jimmy also was asked to dinner by Anthony "Abbie Shots" Abbattemarco and Alphonse "Allie Boy" Persico, the brother of jailed mobster boss Carmine "The Snake" Persico. The main topic of discussion was Mike Rizzi, who was born and bred in Brooklyn, but was presently working for the West Coast mob.

"Have you made Mike Rizzi yet?" Abbie Shots said.

"Not yet," Jimmy said. "But I proposed him, and he'll get made in the next few weeks or so."

"You better make him," Allie Boy said. "If you don't we'll call him back to New York and make him in our family. Mike's a damn good man, and we should have never let him go west in the first place."

One afternoon, while Jimmy was at the Westchester Premier Theater going over the strategies in place, Alphonse D'Ambrosio introduced Jimmy as amico nostra to "Benny Eggs" Mangano, a captain in the Genovese crime family.

"Listen, Jimmy," Benny Eggs said. "I have a clothing store downtown Manhattan that I use as my office. Why don't you come over tomorrow, and I'll introduce to Funzi. Fat Tony will be there too."

Jimmy thought that was a wonderful idea.

Funzi was Frank Tieri, a 74-year-old mob legend, who, in 1972, had ordered the murder of Tommy Eboli, the underboss to Vito Genovese, three years after Genovese passed away in prison. After Genovese's death, Eboli was designated by the Five Family Commission as the acting boss. But with the backing of Carlo Gambino, Funzi was allowed to pull the plug on Eboli, after which Gambino anointed Funzi the head of the Genovese crime family.

"Fat Tony" Salerno was the ailing Funzi's street boss and second-in-command.

The next day, Jimmy and Benny Eggs arrived at the Resource Sales Corporation at 137 Varick Street, just off Spring Street and three blocks from the entrance to the Holland Tunnel. Fat Tony was sitting at a desk in a room at the back of the store, smoking his ever-present Cuban cigar.

Benny Eggs made the proper introductions.

"I want to tell you that Tony Dope from Cleveland sent his regards," Jimmy told Fat Tony.

Fat Tony blew a smoke ring over Jimmy's right shoulder.

"Yeah, tell Tony Dope we're here for anything he might need in the future," Fat Tony said.

"I'm sure Tony Dope will be glad to hear that," Jimmy said. "There's a gang war going on in Cleveland with a bunch of Irish maniacs, and they haven't made guys in years in Cleveland. There's no new blood to fight in the trenches."

"Yeah, that's what I heard," Fat Tony said. "But don't worry. I can send a battalion of capable guys to Cleveland in case they're needed."

Jimmy said his goodbye to Fat Tony, and Benny Eggs took Jimmy to a dumpy little café on Prince Street a few doors down from Broadway. The joint had four small tables and eight stools at a coffee-stained counter. Not a customer was in sight.

But a shriveled old man sat at a back table by himself. He was wearing a cashmere coat with a matching scarf, and he had a fedora crunched on his head and covering one eye. It was the middle of May in New York City, but the old man was dressed for winter in Chicago.

Benny Eggs introduced Jimmy to Funzi Tieri, who had recently undergone an operation for throat cancer. The introduction complete, Benny Eggs made an excuse to exit the premises.

"Tell me what's going on in California," Funzi said to Jimmy. "I hear things are a mess out there. No organization and no coordination since Jack Dragna passed away; just a bunch of cowboys running around with no supervision."

"That's why I was brought into the picture," Jimmy said. "The boss and underboss, Brooklier and Sciortino, are in the can. Me and Louie Dragna are running things until they get out. But I'm in

San Francisco, and it's hard for me to get a handle on things in Los Angeles. We don't have too many guys who are capable and earners. So I'm doing this and that, and scheming all over the place to bring some money into our pockets."

"I heard some of you guys are in contact with Joe Bonanno," Funzi said. "A guy named 'The Weasel' is supposed to be talking with Bonanno. That's against commission rules. We voted this guy out, but we allowed him to live. Still, Bonanno's on the shelf, and he's not even an amico nostra anymore."

Jimmy almost swallowed his tongue.

"They call me 'The Weasel.' But I ain't never met Joe Bonanno in my life," Jimmy said. "If he walked into this joint right now, I wouldn't recognize him. We're having problems with one guy who's running his mouth off, and I heard he's been talking to Bonanno."

"What's his name?" Funzi said.

"Frank Bompensiero," Jimmy said. "He's been warned already, but it doesn't look like he's listening."

"Okay," Funzi said. "You've got to run your family the best way you see fit. But this Bonanno is a leper. Anyone who touches him gets poisoned. Talk to this Bomper..... whatever the fuck his name is. Do this personally. If he doesn't listen, then he's got to get clipped."

Jimmy exited the café with smoke coming out of his ears. Bomp had to be the guy who said "The Weasel" was working with Bonanno. But with a million things on his mind, Jimmy put

In early June, 1976, Jimmy finally got around to making Mike Rizzi an *amico nostra*. Jimmy figured, after his conversations in New York City with Allie Shots and Allie Boy Persico, he better get cracking soon or he's lose Rizzi to the boys from Brooklyn. And quite frankly, besides Jimmy and Bomp, Rizzi was the only other guy on the West Coast capable of being a fighting soldier against the enemy.

To show how shoddy things had become on the West Coast, a Murrieta Hot Springs coffee shop was selected to be the place of Rizzi's induction. Jimmy and Dragna, as co-acting bosses were present, as was Frank Bompensiero, who had recently been upped to *consigliere*. Bomp was especially important to Rizzi's induction since he was the only mobster left on the West Coast who was conversant in the Sicilian dialogue, which was mandatory for this type of ceremony.

"Mike, we're going to give you the quickie version of the deal," Jimmy said.

"But we've got to put the gun and the knife in front of Mike," Bomp said. "We can't do that here in a public place."

Jimmy shrugged his shoulders and turned to Bomp

"I figured you were going to say that," Jimmy said.

"Hey, what's right is right," Bomp said. "It's no good without the knife and the gun. And don't forget about the burning saint picture."

The four men got up from the table, exited the restaurant, and jumped into Dragna's Caddy parked out front. Rizzi sat in the front with Dragna, and Jimmy and Bomp sat in the back with the gun and the knife, and the photo of the saint which had not yet been ignited.

Dragna took the highway out of town, and about a half hour later, he hung a right onto a deserted dirt road. The four men got out of the car and stepped right into a heavy drizzle. As Bomp muttered a bastardized version of the Sicilian induction dialogue, Jimmy placed the gun and the knife on the hood of the car. Louie Dragna dropped a photo of a saint in Mike Rizzi cupped hands, and with the rain coming down heavier, he tried to fire up a match. It took Dragna four tries, but he finally married the match's flame to the photo of the saint.

Amongst other things, Rizzi agreed that if he ever betrayed his crime family, he should burn like the saint's photo is his hands.

Jimmy used safety pin to prick Rizzi's finger, and after more clipped Sicilian chatter by Bomp, Mike Rizzi was formally inducted into the Italian Mob, or "The Mafia" as the news media and law enforcement incorrectly label the organization (P.S. – The real Mafia exists only in Sicily).

The four men hugged and kissed and patted backs all around.

"You are now one of us," Jimmy said to Rizzi. "Congratulations, *amico nostra*."

Bomp wiped the top of his bald head with his right hand.

"Let's get the fuck out of here before I get pneumonia," Bomp said.

And that's what they did.

To Jimmy's dismay, on July 28, 1976, the mob finally disposed of Johnny Roselli; and not in a very nice way.

At the time of his death, Roselli was still living in Miami, and therefore in the jurisdiction of old Miami mobster, Santo Trafficante, who according to Roselli, was also involved in the mob discussions with the CIA to rub out Fidel Castro. Roselli, 71-years-old, was visiting his daughter's home in Plantation, and when he left, he told her that he was going to have dinner with his old pal, Santo.

Roselli was never again seen alive.

On August 8, 1976, Roselli's decomposed body was found by three fisherman floating in a 55-gallon steel drum in five feet of water in Dumfounding Bay, in Eastern Shores, Florida, which is within the city limits of the City of North Miami. Mostly likely because rigor mortis had already set in, Roselli's legs were cut off and stuffed into the drum next to his torso. Although there were several knife wounds in Roselli face and torso, the coroner said the cause of death was asphyxiation.

The headline in the August 23, 1976 issue of *Time Magazine* read:

Deep Six for Johnny

The article led with:

> *Roselli was one of a dying breed that is dying off, usually by murder.*
>
> *They buried him in the classic style. His body was sealed in an empty 55-galon oil drum. Heavy chains were coiled around the container, and holes were punched in the sides. Then the drum was dumped in the waters off Florida. It might have stayed on the bottom indefinitely—except that the gases caused by the decomposing body gave the drum buoyancy and floated it to the surface.*

Roselli's body was discovered just two months after Roselli had testified for the third time in front of the U.S. Select Committee on Intelligence, which was headed by Idaho Senator Frank Church. The purpose of the committee was to delve into the possibility that the Mafia had teamed up with the CIA to kill Fidel Castro. Also implicated in this alleged plot was Santo Trafficante, which led law enforcement to believe that Trafficante was responsible for Roselli's demise. United States Attorney General Edward Levi immediately instructed the FBI to determine if Roselli had been murdered because of his testimony.

But dig as they may, the FBI founded no evidence involving Trafficante in Roselli's demise. Trafficante ruled Florida until March 17, 1987, when he died at the ripe old age of 72 at the Texas Heart Institute in Houston, where he had gone for heart surgery.

Two weeks after Roselli's body was found, Jimmy took a trip to Chicago to see the Chicago Outfit boss, Joey Aiuppa. The meeting was ostensibly to discuss the mob war going on in Cleveland for control of the otherworld rackets. Aiuppa, knowing Jimmy was from Cleveland and was close to several Cleveland mobsters, wanted to know if Jimmy knew someone who could be of help in eliminating a Cleveland Irish psycho named Danny Greene.

Roselli and Aiuppa sat in the back of a mobbed-up Chicago bistro and had a few scotches, while on the juke box Sinatra was telling them to bring in the clowns.

"Fucking Sinatra, we should have clipped him when the Kennedys fucked us in the ass," Aiuppa said. "We help that fuck JFK get elected president, and then he sics his faggot brother Bobby on us. Fuck, they pulled Carlo Marcello out his bed in the middle of the night and put him on a plane to Guatemala; said he was an undesirable alien or something. Sinatra was supposed to handle the Kennedys, but he fucked up and we got hurt bad."

"So, how come you didn't clip Sinatra?" Jimmy said. "He ain't too popular with the press. You could have made it looked like an accident, like they did with Marilyn Monroe."

"Nah, fuck, we weren't worried about the press or any shit like that," Aiuppa said. "It was Sam. He was the boss then. He said he didn't want to have Sinatra clipped because he liked the way Sinatra sang 'Chicago – My Kind of Town.' I think that was bullshit. Sinatra was getting Sam so much pussy, Sam couldn't afford to lose him."

Then out of nowhere, Aiuppa started taping the side of his head with the tips of his fingers, like he was trying to recall something.

"By the way, do you remember that guy, what the fuck's his name, that they found in a barrel in Florida?" Aiuppa said.

Jimmy's anger was too intense to answer.

The Aiuppa snapped his fingers, like he just had remembered.

"Yeah, now I recall the guy I was referring to," Aiuppa said. "His name was Johnny Roselli. He used to be a friend of Sam's. You remember him, don't you?"

By this time the two gangster's eyes had locked onto each other's, and they weren't flirting.

Aiuppa was obviously enjoying this, and he wanted to get a rise out of Jimmy, so that he's have a reason to clip him too.

Jimmy grinded his teeth, and said, "Yeah, I remember him."

"So what do you think of that?" Aiuppa said.

Jimmy took a deep breath, and he shrugged his shoulders. Jimmy knew how to play this game better than Aiuppa.

"What's there to think?" Jimmy said. "It's one of those things. He's dead. Things like that happened all the time in this thing of ours."

Aiuppa leaned forward, and Jimmy could smell the booze on his breath.

"You know I just got appointed on the National Commission, don't you?" Aiuppa said.

Jimmy smiled, and said, "Yes, of course I know. I'm the acting boss on the West Coast. I'm told things like that right away. Congratulations."

"I'm glad you feel like that," Aiuppa said. "We wouldn't want any problems."

"Nah, this Roselli stuff is your business; not mine," Jimmy said. "I'm back on the West Coast and I got my own problems."

Now, Jimmy knew the deal for sure. Aiuppa had both Giancana and Roselli whacked, and since Jimmy was close to both men, Aiuppa wanted to send a message that Jimmy could be next.

Jimmy left the meeting with Aiuppa with a heavy heart. But he thanked God he had gotten transferred back to the West Coast mob when he had. Otherwise, he might be dead already.

Jimmy knew things usually happened in threes, and less than two weeks after Roselli's murder he got a phone call from "Tony Dope" Delsanter in Cleveland.

"Jimmy, I need you here right way," Tony Dope said. "I can't talk on the phone, but you know me. I don't ask for favors unless it's really something important."

Without question, Jimmy took the next plane to Cleveland. After his plane landed, he grabbed a cab to Sabbatino's Restaurant on in Cleveland's Little Italy. Tony Dope was sitting at his customary table in the back. Tony Dope stood up and kissed Jimmy on both cheeks.

Then he whispered into Jimmy ear, "Let's go for a little walk. This place is bugged. As soon as we find one bug, the feds put in another one. Those fucks don't even use a warrant anymore."

Jimmy and Tony Dope exited Sabbatino's and headed east on Mayfield Road.

Tony Dope put his arm around Jimmy and whispered into his ear, "We lost Leo (Moceri) a few days ago. He just disappeared, and the last time he was seen alive he was with John Nardi."

"John Nardi?" Jimmy said. "He's not even a made guy."

"Neither is that Irishman fuck Danny Greene," Tony Dope said. "But they're both trying to kill us off so that they can take over everything here in Cleveland. We need young blood out in Cleveland. I'd ask you to jump in and help us, but I know you've got your hands filled on the West Coast."

"Why don't you just make some new guys?" Jimmy said. "You must have some capable men who are just dying to get their buttons."

"Yeah, who?" Tony Dope said. "And even if we did have the right people in mind, fuck, we haven't made new guys in 30 years. None of us even know the right words, or nothing for the ceremony."

"Don't worry," Jimmy said. "You find the guys, and I'll come down and do the induction. And besides, all you have to do is call Chicago or New York and they'll send you all the shooters you need to handle the situation."

"Yeah, I know that," Tony Dope said." But I've spoken to Blackie (Cleveland mob boss Jack Licavoli), and he wants us to take care of our own family business."

"Well, how about Ray Ferritto from Erie, Pennsylvania?" Jimmy said. "I did time with him in Chino. He's a very capable guy. And he's looking to get his button. But nobody is doing anything for him in Erie. If you want, I can reach out to him for you."

"Yeah, that's a good idea," Tony Dope said. "I know he's a good friend of Ronnie Carabbia, and I know his reputation. Get in touch with him for me. Tell him I'll make it worth his while."

In September of 1976, Jimmy, after making a quick stop in Cleveland to induct two new mob members, traveled back to Westchester, New York, to take in Frank Sinatra's final show at the Westchester Premier Theater. There, Jimmy met with all the old gang involved in the theater's shenanigans, including Carlo Gambino, who was obviously the man in charge.

After Sinatra's show, the gangsters were all seated at a long table in the theater's dining room enjoying their prime rib dinner. At the head of the table was old man, Gambino, and sitting at his right hand was his cousin and future successor, "Big Paul" Castellano. Besides Jimmy, also at the table were Greg DePalma, Richie Fusco, Joe Gambino - Carlo's nephew, and "Fat Tommy" Marson, who looked like had had just swallowed a basketball.

After dinner was done, one of Gambino's flunkies came over to the table and whispered into the old man's ears.

Gambino raised his right hand, and all talking at the table ceased.

"Alright, now it's time we go see Frank backstage," Gambino said.

The entire crew absconded to Sinatra's dressing room, where Sinatra was gracious enough to take a group phto with all of them included. This photo would make most of the participants cringe, when it was admitted into evidence during several future mob trials.

After everyone, but Jimmy, glad-handed Sinatra, Marson introduced Jimmy to The Chairman of the Board. Jimmy had met Sinatra several times 30 years earlier in Las Vegas, when Sinatra's Adam's apple was greater than his song list.

"Sure, I remember you," Sinatra said to Jimmy. "I hear you're on top of the heap on the West Coast where me and Tommy live."

"That's only for the time being," Jimmy said. "But if there's anything I can do for you, don't hesitate to ask."

"There is something you can do for me," Sinatra said. "When we're all back in California, I'll have Jilly Rizzo speak to you."

"Fine," Jimmy said.

The next day Jimmy made a trip to the little café on the Lower East Side of Manhattan to meet again with Funzi Tieri. The old man was sitting in the same spot in the cafe, wearing the same overcoat, and the same hat when Jimmy last saw him. And it was 60 degrees in September.

Funzi invited Jimmy to sit, and after the waiter placed a cup of espresso in front of Jimmy along with a bottle of Marie Brizard anisette, Funzi said, "Okay, tell me about the situation in Cleveland. I know you're close with those guys."

"Things are pretty bad in Cleveland," Jimmy said. "We lost Leo Moceri a few weeks back."

"Yeah, I heard," Funzi said. "And all of us can't let this go unpunished. Leo was an underboss, and these disgraziatas who did this thing are not even made men. And one of them is a fucking Irishman. This is fucking unheard of! Tell Jack Licavoli, if he needs any help, let me know. I want these guys whacked. The sooner, the better."

"Thanks, I will," Jimmy said. "But Blackie wants the Cleveland mob to handle this on their own. I already gave them a good man in Ray Ferritto."

"I heard they finally made two new guys in Cleveland," Funzi said.

"Yeah, I did the ceremony myself," Jimmy said. "I made Tony Liberatore and John Calandra; two good men I've known for years."

"Good, since you're the acting boss in California, I'd like you to come to a sitdown tomorrow at Benny Eggs's office in the Village, Funzi said. "We're deciding if a certain scumbag gets hit or not, and he happens to be on the lam in your jurisdiction in California. All my keys guys will be there."

"Sure," Jimmy said. "Do you mind if I bring Mike Rizzi? I just made him a captain."

"Sure, bring Mike," Funzi said. "I've heard only good things about him."

The following day Jimmy and Rizzi sat at a large round table in the back of Benny Eggs's clothing store. According to *The Last Mafioso*, also sitting at the table was Carmine "Eli" Zeccardi - Funzi's underboss, Fat Tony Salerno - Funzi's consigliere, and Funzi's top captain, Vincent "Chin" Gigante. Jimmy was honored to be at a sitdown involving New York's City's finest goodfellows.

Funzi turned to Jimmy, and said, "Jimmy, the reason I invited you is that this concerns somebody in your territory. Chin will tell you all about it."

Chin Gigante took Funzi's baton and ran with it.

"This guy, Joe (Joseph Spencer) Ullo stuck me for a bundle of shylock money, and he skipped out to California," Gigante said. "So we sent this guy, Gazut (Vincent Calderazzo), to collect my money and now Gazut's missing. So we figured Ullo thought Gazut was going to clip him, so he hit him first and buried the body."

Jimmy described what happened next in *Vengeance is Mine*:

"Then Gigante asked me if I knew of a guy named Ullo. I told him, no, I didn't know him. I asked Mike (Rizzi) if he ever heard of the guy, and Mike says he never heard of him either. So Funzi then said, 'Okay now we've got to vote, and I vote hit.' Then Gigante said, 'I vote hit too.' And he pointed his right thumb down on the table. Then Salerno and Eli both pointed their thumbs down and said, 'Hit.' So it was unanimous. This guy Ullo had to get clipped."

Funzi stood up, indicating the sitdown was over.

"That it," Funzi said. "Send somebody out there right away."

"Listen, Funzi. Is you need any help, I'll give the Chin Rizzi's phone number," Jimmy said. "Chin can call Mike anytime."

Fortunately for Ullo, the California state police caught Ullo before the mob did. Ullo was already wanted for the Los Angeles murder of gambler Jack Molinas, a Brooklynite who was involved in the 1957 college basketball point-shaving scandal. Ullo was tried for Molinas's murder, but was found not guilty because of the scant evidence.

As for Calderazzo (Gazut), two informants led the police to Calderazzo's gave in the desert. Ullo was charged with his murder too, but the judge dismissed the case because two of the witnesses against him had perjured themselves.

There is no record of Chin Gigante's crew every carrying out the hit out on Ullo.

However, Jimmy Fratianno, the acting boss in California, was present when the hierarchy of the Genovese crime family approved a mob murder, and this would come back to haunt the New York crew later.

Jimmy was dying to meet the former "Miss Australia," Eve Markovics, but when he met her father, Ivan, dollar signs began flicking before his eyes.

Ivan Markovics, a shady character if there ever was one, was influential in "The Knights of Malta," a secretive religious order with a long and bloody history and unique status under international law.

It was an old friend and fellow crook, Rudy Tham, an officer of the Teamsters, who told Jimmy all about Markovics and the con he was running.

"This Knights of Malta is such an exclusive organization, you have to be sponsored by a member and approved by the Vatican in Rome to become a member," Tham said. "But this guy Markovics, for the right price, cuts through all the red tape in Rome. Besides all his expenses, anyone who wants to get in has to donate ten grand to the organization itself."

"That sounds like a high class scam to me," Jimmy said.

"Maybe it is a scam, but people are dying to get in this exclusive organization," Tham said. "Lot of famous people already are members. Kings, Queens, ambassadors and even presidents in Europe belong."

Jimmy could care less about joining such an organization, much less pay money to get in. But he knew someone who would give just about anything to get inducted – his old and new pal, Frank Sinatra.

Tham and Jimmy met Ivan and Eve Markovics at a party given by the Teamsters. Eve was absolutely beautiful, with dark brown hair, almond-shaped eyes and olive skin. Jimmy was only slight disappointed when he discovered she was not "Miss Australia," but in fact, had finished third in the beauty contest.

At this party, Jimmy cornered Ivan Markovics and asked for the lowdown on the Knights of Malta.

"Who's the top man in the outfit?" Jimmy said.

"Every country has its own chapter," Ivan said. "There's one in France, Italy, Germany and England. And there's even one in American that over 100 years old.'

"I heard you can go to Rome and get somebody made," Jimmy said.

"That's partially true," Ivan said. "There's Price Petrucci. He's the Prince of Italy – the head of the Italian chapter.'

"What about the Pope?" Jimmy said. "Doesn't he have any say-so in this?"

Ivan smiled and said, "The Pope actually has nothing to do with our organization. But the Prince works with the Cardinals, and when we have an investor, he brings over a couple of Cardinals and we have quite an induction ceremony. For a thousand years the Knights of Malta has been one of the most exclusive social orders in the world. And the Maltese Cross, which is given for outstanding accomplishments in various fields and services to humanity, is one of the most prestigious awards in the world. In over a thousand years, only seven hundred people have received it."

Now Jimmy saw his opening to make some significant cash.

"Do you sometimes have fund raisers to get more money for the organization?" Jimmy said.

"Yes, we often do, but it's hard to get the biggest starts to contribute their time," Ivan said.

"Well, is Frank Sinatra, the greatest singer in the world, a big enough star for you?" Jimmy said.

"Oh, of course," Ivan said. "Do you know him?"

"Absolutely, Frank's a good friend of mine," Jimmy said. "If you can get Frank inducted into the Knights of Malta, I'll get him to star in a big benefit for the Knights of Malta. But the way it works is this. You get Frank inducted, and then I'll get him to do the benefits. This is all cash and carry, understand?"

Ivan Markovics said he certainly did understand.

In Frank Sinatra's world, everything goes through his California lawyer, Mickey Rudin. At an after-show party at the Rainbow Room in Manhattan, Jimmy, who was in town again for one of Sinatra's shows at the Westchester Premier Theater, approached Rudin about Ivan Markovics's plan to make Sinatra a Knight of Malta. Sinatra and his wife, Barbara, had just arrived, and Jimmy decided to make his pitch to Rudin.

"All you need to give Ivan Markovics is five grand up front for expenses, and he'll get the ball rolling for Frank," Jimmy said.

"Yeah, I know all about this Ivan Markovics and his beautiful daughter," Rudin said. "But if you ask me, it's all a scam."

Jimmy lowered his voice into a growl.

"Shut your fucking mouth, you cocksucker," Jimmy said. "This is no scam, and this guy is no phony. Furthermore, we don't want your fucking money, so shove it up your ass."

Rudin looked like he was about to faint.

"Look, I didn't mean it that way," Rudin said.

"Fuck, you didn't, you prick," Jimmy said. "I would never try to con Frank out of a dime. I never pull scams on my friends. Now shut the fuck up and walk away from me. I'll be in touch when I have all the details."

Rudin slithered away like he was carrying a load in the seat of his pants.

Two weeks later, Jimmy phoned Rudin at his Los Angeles office.

"The fix is in," Jimmy told Rudin. "Tell Frank that Ivan's coming over to Tommy Marson's place at Rancho Mirage. There we can make the final arrangements."

"That's great," Rudin said. "When will this happen?"

"Next week, sometime," Jimmy said. "I'll call the day before to confirm."

The following week, Frank Sinatra made the trip on foot from his house on the Rancho Mirage golf course to Marson's, 200 yards down the road, or a solid five-iron shot. When he arrived, already present were Markovics and his daughter, Eve, Rudin, Sinatra's personal body guard, Jilly Rizzo, Jimmy, and Frank Bomp.

Markovics was all decked out in the official costume of the Knights of Malta: red silk, robe and the Maltese Cross dangling from a gold rope chain on his neck. He presented Sinatra with the official scroll of the Knights of Malta, a red silk box containing two gold medals and a red flag with the Maltese Cross embroidered on it. He also gave Sinatra a red passport, with the Maltese Cross stamped on the front, inside, and back of the passport.

"This is not an international passport," Markovics told Sinatra. "But it is very respected in all the European countries. You will get special courtesies when you present this passport at European airports."

Sinatra smiled, and said, "So if I try to smuggle hot diamonds into Europe, this passport won't help."

"I'm afraid not," Mr. Sinatra," Markovics said.

Markovics then made arrangement for Sinatra's official induction ceremony.

"I'm looking at early next year, January or February," Markovics said. "Prince Bernhard of Holland would like to attend if his transportation and lodging can be arranged. There are other American members who will also like to attend to welcome you into the Sacred Order. We need to provide for them also"

"No problem," Sinatra said. "I'll have my private jet handle everything at LaGuardia Airport. And they can all stay here at the Canyon Hotel in Palm Springs. I'll take care of that too."

After Sinatra finished with Markovics, Jimmy and Frank Bomp cornered Sinatra out by the pool.

"Frank, now we need a favor from you," Jimmy said. "Our family is not doing good financially, and the Knights of Malta is basically broke because the last guy in charge robbed them blind. So we need you to do a benefit, maybe two nights, for all of us the next time you're appearing at the Westchester Premier Theater."

"That's no problem, Jimmy" Sinatra said. "All we have to do is add two shows to my next trip. Get in touch with Greg DePalma to work out all the details. You can always use Mickey Rudin to get in touch with me. If you have a problem with Mickey, and I know he can be a pain in the ass sometimes, get in touch with Jilly Rizzo. He'll tell me what's going on, and I'll straighten out Mickey for you."

"Fine, Frank, that's works out okay," Jimmy said.

"One thing, Jimmy," Sinatra said. "I need a little favor from you here in California. Jilly will be in touch with you later with the details."

A few days later, while Jimmy was slurping pina coladas at Tommy Marson's place, Jilly came over for a visit.

"Let's talk outside," Jilly told Jimmy. "This place could be bugged."

The two men went for a stroll on the golf course, and Jilly got right to the point.

"Jimmy there's this guy named Andy Celantano that's giving Frank a big problem," Jilly said. "Andy, his nickname is Banjo, used to work for Frank as a bodyguard. But he was always getting soused on the job and going broke at the track. So Frank fired him. Now this guy's threatening to go to the Hollywood scandal sheets to dish some dirt on Frank; you know, saying things like Frank has mobster friends and all that other bullshit."

"Okay, I get the setup, now what do you want me to do about it?" Jimmy said. "You want the guy clipped and it's done."

"Nah, Frank don't want to the guy dead, just busted up," Jilly said. "Break his arms and legs, and put him in the hospital."

"Okay, where can I find this guy?" Jimmy said.

"That's the problem," Jilly said. "I can't find Banjo. And I don't have the time to drop everything and just go looking for this guy. I figure he's either in Burbank or Glendale. And if he's there, he's at the race tracks. I'll get you pictures of him. Have your guys hang out at the tracks till you spot him."

"Okay, tell Frank we'll do what he wants," Jimmy said. "But tell him without an address, it might take some time."

Jimmy put Mike Rizzi on the case, but he never even got a sniff of Banjo.

In October of 1977, Andy "Banjo" Celantano died of a heart attack, and Jimmy "The Wesel" Fratianno never got the chance to do that special favor for Frank Sinatra.

As for the Knights of Malta testimonial starring Frank Sinatra, it never happened.

On January, 9, 1977, Sinatra's mother, Dolly, 82, perished in a plane crash after the light plane, in which she was a passenger, crashed into the 11,592 foot Mount San Giorgio after leaving Palm Springs Municipal Airport. Sinatra wanted to be inducted in the Knights of Malta only to please his mother. Dolly Sinatra's death made Frank's induction into the Knights of Malta, and the testimonial concert to line Jimmy's pockets with cash, pointless as far as Frank Sinatra was concerned.

The beginning of the end of Jimmy "The Weasel" Fratianno's life as a mobster took place in late October of 1976, when Dominick Brooklier was released from prison after serving sixteen months, mostly in the prison hospital.

A month later, Brooklier, looking feeble and emaciated, summoned Jimmy and Mike Rizzi for a meeting in Brooklier's son, Anthony's, law office. After the customary hellos all around, Brooklier took Jimmy alone into a side office. This is where Jimmy told Brooklier all the about the deals with Sinatra, and he promised Brooklier a piece of the skims on Sinatra's Knights of Malta benefit dinner at the Westchester Premier Theater.

Jimmy got his first hint of trouble ahead when Brooklier told him, "You know, Sam Sciortino is ready to get back into action as the family's underboss. I want you to introduce this Jilly Rizzo to Sam. From this point on, I want Sam to be our point man in the dealings with Sinatra."

After agreeing to make Jimmy's man, Mike Rizzi, a captain, Brooklier also told Jimmy, "And you can forget about clipping Bomp. We got a few good men on the job: Tommy Ricciardi and this Tony "The Ant" Spilotro, who's doing a lot of work in Las Vegas for the Chicago mob. But I may need you to make a few calls to Bomp when we're ready to set him up. You know, make him feel comfortable to go to certain pay phone. Things like that."

In late 1976, The feds launched a phony pornographic distributor in California called Forex. Then they contacted Frank "Bomp" Bompensiero and convinced him to get his buddies, including Jimmy "The Weasel" Fratianno, to shake down Forex, because they were "operating in our territory." Jimmy didn't like the idea – the Forex guys just appeared out of thin air. But Louie Dragna was all for it and so was Brooklier. So, they sent Mike Rizzi, Tommy Ricciardi and Jack LoCicero to talk to Forex about kicking up some big bucks to the California mob.

In February 1977, the feds lowered the boom on the Forex extorters. Indictments were handed down to Bomp (as a ruse), Rizzi, Ricciardi, LoCicero and Jimmy, who was especially pissed off because he hadn't trusted the setup in the first place, and he had told Bomp to explicitly keep him name out of the entire deal.

Jimmy phoned his old pal Bomp, who by now everyone in the California mob was convinced was an FBI informant.

"Who the fuck was that guy who pitched you Forex?" Jimmy said.

Bomp tried to play dumb.

"Which guy? What the fuck you talking about?" Bump said.

"You know which guy, you cocksucker," Jimmy said. "That Forex bullshit was an FBI undercover operation. Now, who the fuck is the guy who gave you the fucking tip?"

"Oh shit, it was just some guy who owns a porno shop in San Diego," Bomp said. "Let me check this out, and I'll get back to you."

According to *The Last Mafioso*, Bomp called Jimmy back two days later.

"Hey, Jimmy, you know that guy you was asking about?" Bomp said. "Well, he's Bye-Bye Blackbird."

Obviously, Bomp thought Jimmy was stupid enough to buy the lie that Bomp had killed the guy who tipped Bomp to Forex, when Jimmy knew damn well that it was the FBI.

"Okay, Bomp, I get you," Jimmy said. "You better cover your tracks. If it was a setup, they'll be looking for this motherfucker."

"Don't worry, everything's cool," Bomp said. 'I got this fucking situation under control."

A few weeks later, Bomp, and the others who were indicted, were called by the feds to Los Angeles to testify before a grand jury about the Forex extortion. Jimmy took the Fifth Amendment to avoid incriminating himself.

As was reported in *A Bad, Bad, Boy – The Most Feared Mobster in California in 30 Years* by Judith Moore, Jim Holman and Sandy Huffake, an FBI agent who often surveilled Bomp said, "Bompensiero's behavior began during this time to change. Frank had never been much of a drinker. But during this period, he began to drink a lot. About a week before the grand jury was to meet, he was at lunch at Tarantino's Restaurant in Point Loma. He ordered a mixed drink with a beer back. He was loud, which Frank never really was. He was going, 'Yeah, canary, tweet, tweet,' alluding to the fact that there was an informant, that someone had snitched him off. He was extremely loud. He was actually obnoxious.

"I followed him after he left the place. His lawyer, DePento, was in the passenger seat. Bompensiero was driving about 55 mph in the Mustang. He almost hit the center divider. He was in those days very flushed. He must have been feeling very pressured. I saw a complete change in personality and actions. He was extremely nervous.

"I followed Bompensiero to Los Angeles. When Bompensiero and the other Los Angeles family members arrived at the federal courthouse, Bompensiero was standing separate from the other guys. They were rather distinctly away from him on the steps. They kept to themselves, which at the time I thought very interesting. They were inconspicuously away from him. There was just Frank and his attorney, DePento, on the steps."

Two days later, Jimmy met with Brooklier and his underboss, Sam Sciortino, at a Los Angeles golf course. They picked up their golf carts at the cart barn and drove to the clubhouse where they parked in the lot outside.

Sciortino told Jimmy, "This guy (Bomp) is a lying son-of-a-bitch. We ought to kill him."

Jimmy said, "Yeah, Bomp is a wrong guy and he's no good. We got to do something about him. He's an informant. No doubt about it now."

Brooklier shook Jimmy's hand, and said, "Thanks for all the help with this, Jimmy. We'll take it from here. And we'll be in touch."

On the morning of February 10, 1977, on the orders of Brooklier through Tommy Ricciardi, Jimmy, from a pay phone at the San Francisco Hilton, called Bomp at a designated phone booth in San Diego near the luxurious Pacific Beach apartments where Bomp lived with his wife under the name "Frank Gavin." The two mobsters made small talk, mostly about how Brooklier had taken over the West Coast mob and kicked them to the curb. They agreed to talk again on the phone, either later in the day or on the following day.

A few days earlier, the feds were tailing Bomp when they saw a suspicious car following Bomp. The feds stormed the car, and they found two mugs with shotguns sitting on their laps. The two played dumb, and the feds arrested them for carrying illegal firearms.

The report got back to Bomp's FBI handler, Jack Armstrong. Armstrong, who had already offered Bomp the Witness Protection Program, but was shunned, contacted Bomp and told him there was definitely a contract on his life.

"Bomp, I think it's time we pulled you off the streets," Armstrong said.

"Fuck that," Bomp said. "I know this game better than all of them. Nobody's getting to me and that's that."

On the night of February 10, Frank "Bomp" Bompensiero made one phone call too many.

Bomp had exited the Pacific Beach Apartments, his pockets filled with dimes and nickels. As soon as he dropped his first coin at the phone booth at an Arco gas station, a man emerged from the shadows and pumped four 22 caliber bullets from a gun with a silencer into Frank Bompensiero's head. After ascertaining Bomp was indeed dead, the gunman jumped into the passenger seat of a dark sedan, and the wheelman peeled away.

Jimmy Fratianno was dining at Count Montefusco's restaurant with Skinny Vellota when an associate named Sal Amarena busted in and told them Bomp had been shot dead at a San Diego phone booth. After he turned rat, Jimmy told the feds that it was Tommy Ricciardi who had been the shooter, and the getaway driver was Jack LoCicero.

Fratianno said that Ricciardi had told him, "You know, when I clipped Bomp he gave me a little struggle. But it was beautiful. There was no noise. It went along beautiful."

Soon after Frank Bompensiero was whacked, Jimmy was summoned to a meeting with Brooklier and his underboss Sciortino at a condo owned by Sciortino's cousin.

The three men sat alone in the living room, and Jimmy could feel the hatred permeating from both men's pores.

"Listen Jimmy, I heard there's two factions of my crew; mine and yours," Brooklier said. "What do you have to say about that?"

"What the fuck are you getting at?" Jimmy said. "You're the one who told me to hold things together while you were in the can, and that's what I did."

"Yeah, but I hear you've been presently yourself all around the country as the boss of the West Coast mob," Brooklier said. "Things like that get back to me. And when I told the other bosses the truth, they didn't like it either. You got a big mouth, Jimmy, and it's going to get you into trouble."

"Look, I transferred from Chicago to help you guys out when Louie asked me," Jimmy said. "There's nothing in L.A. I want. The whole fucking town is yours. I'm staying in San Francisco."

"Your living in San Francisco makes no difference," Brooklier said. "You're still a soldier in my family, and I'm still your boss."

"Not if I go back to Chicago where I rightfully should be," Jimmy said. "I only came out here because you guys basically begged me."

Jimmy was hot. He pointed to Sciortino.

"And where did you find this prick?" Jimmy said. "He's got no balls, and he's been poisoning your mind against me."

"Sam's my underboss. Show him some respect," Brooklier said.

"Yeah, so you say," Jimmy said.

It was Sciortino's turn to pipe in.

"You know we eliminated Bomp," Sciortino said. "And there's more to come."

"Are you threatening me, you piece of shit?" Jimmy said.

"I'll explain what Sam meant," Brooklier said. "There ain't going to be any more bullshit around the family like there was in the past. Anyone who doesn't chalk the line is going to be hit in the head."

Brooklier's mouth transformed into an evil grin.

"You know I was the one who made the call to Bomp that sent him to that phone booth," Brooklier said. "That's the way it going to be from now on. No more bullshit."

"I hear you loud and clear," Jimmy said. "And I don't like what I'm hearing; just threats. No thank yous for all I done for you guys while you were in jail."

Having said his piece, Jimmy stormed from the room and slammed the door behind him.

The May 16, 1977 issue of *Time Magazine* ran this headline on the front page:

The Mafia – Big Bad and Booming

The first paragraph said:

> *New Orleans Mafia Boss Carlos Marcello has doubled his force of bodyguards and shipped his family to a safe haven out of state. New York Don Aniello Dellacroce confuses his enemies by sometimes having a look-alike impersonate him in public. James ("the Weasel") Fratianno, a high-level mobster in San Francisco, rarely goes anywhere without two hulking companions. Other Mafia chieftains start their cars by remote control just in case bombs are wired to the ignitions. Fear has always been a palpable part of life at the top in the Mafia.*

Nowhere in the article does *Time Magazine* even mention the name Dominick Brooklier. However, James "Jimmy the Weasel" Fratianno is give prime space.

The article continues:

> *Fratianno, 62, is believed by police to have made up to 16 hits as the "Mob's West Coast Executioner." When the Gambino and Chicago mobsters decided in 1975 to move into the West they tapped Fratianno as their point man. With their blessing, he recruited Mike Rizzitello, now 50, a handsome stickup artist, who migrated to Los Angeles in the early 1960's because he wanted an easy racket and respect that he never got from the hoodlums back home. Rizzitello helped the Mafia take over 80% of the $100 million-a-year pornography business.*

Jimmy knew this *Time Magazine* article would be read by every mobster capable of reading in the United States of America. And while it felt good to be recognized as such a force by the press, it didn't look good to his FBI handler, Larry Lawrence, who was beginning to feel Jimmy wasn't always telling him the total truth about what illegal activities he was involved with.

In the next day's newspaper, Jimmy found out that someone had planted a bomb in car parked next to the parked car of John Nardi in the parking lot next to the Teamsters building in Cleveland. The bomb exploded and Nardi was dead. Jimmy wondered what was taking so long for the Cleveland mob to get rid of Danny Greene. But Jimmy figured, the less he knew about the Cleveland mob war, the better.

In August 1977, Jimmy good friend, Anthony "Tony Dope" Delsanter died suddenly of a heart attack. Jimmy flew to Cleveland for the funeral. After the wake, Jimmy went to a local Italian social club with Jack "Blackie" Licavoli. As they sat and drank espresso laced with Sambuca, Blackie handed Jimmy a sheet of paper. It contained the names of several FBI informants, including Danny Greene and Frank Bompensiero under the heading, "Cleveland," plus Tony Hughes and Curley Montana under "Chicago." It did not include the name James Fratianno.

"We got a girl secretary who works in the FBI office, and she can get us whatever we need," Tony Dope said. "This sheet of paper proves Bomp was a rat, and that Danny Greene was a rat too."

"Does this broad have access to all the FBI's documents?" Jimmy said.

"You bet your ass she does," Licavoli said. "If you need something special, let me know."

"Yeah, see if you can find out about any rats out on the West Coast," Jimmy said. "I'm sure Bomp wasn't the only one."

"Will do," Licavoli said. "But it might take some time. It's like pulling teeth with this broad."

This news put Jimmy in a very precarious situation. He was basically shoveling FBI Agent Lawrence bullshit stories about the mob, and getting paid a ton of money to do so. But what if the FBI secretary turned over to the Cleveland mob a list of West Coast informants with Jimmy's name on it? This would give Brooklier another reason to put Jimmy six feet under, as if he needed another reason.

Jimmy hadn't spoken to Lawrence for a few months, so he quickly put in a call to him from a pay phone at the San Francisco Hilton.

"Hey pal, I haven't heard from you for a while. What gives?" Jimmy said.

"Oh, I thought you knew," Lawrence said. "I put in my papers a couple of months back. I'm retired. I figured someone from the bureau would have contacted you by now."

"You're shitting me," Jimmy said. "I never heard a word from anyone. And now we have a problem. There's a girl in the Cleveland FBI office who's stealing all kinds of shit. She gave the Cleveland guys a list of informants."

"I'm assuming you weren't on the list," Lawrence said.

"If I was, I'd be dead already," Jimmy said. "But I'll give you the names of two guys: Curley Montana and Tony Hughes. Check this out, and if they really are informants, you know this girl can be dangerous to a lot of guys."

"Okay, I'll make some phone calls," Lawrence said. "Call me tomorrow. We can't waste any time on this."

The next day, when Jimmy called Lawrence he was told to go to the office of James F. Ahern, the Assistant Special Agent in Charge of the San Francisco field FBI office. When he got there, Ahern's assistant, Charles "Chuck" Hiner was also present.

Before Jimmy even sat down, he barked," Who's the main guy in this office? I'm only dealing with the top guy here."

"I'm the second-in-charge of this office," Ahern said. "My boss, Roy McKinnon, is out of town. So if you want immediate action on this, you have to deal with me."

"Well, I don't think you understand," Jimmy said. "I just passed this information on to Larry, and I told him to keep me out of this. My sister and other members of my family live in Cleveland."

"Well, if you want us to plug this leak in the Cleveland office, we're going to need your help," Ahern said.

"Now wait a fucking minute, these guys in Cleveland all know me," Jimmy said. "If I get involved, my family is in danger."

"Did you notice Licavoli's actions when he gave you this information?" Ahern said. "Maybe he was just baiting you to see what you knew. The bottom line is you are already in danger. We know for a fact that the mob here in California has a contract out on you. Besides, the Cleveland FBI office thinks you're full of shit. They don't believe they have a leak inside their office. And I need you to help me convince them that they do."

"Okay, I'll go to Cleveland and see what I can find out," Jimmy said. "I've got to see Licavoli anyway about a Teamsters deal with Jackie Presser. But if this goes to a grand jury or anything, leave me out of this."

"I'll do what I can, Jimmy," Ahearn said. "And while you're out there see if you can find out anything about this gang war with Nardi and Greene."

"I don't know anything about that shit, and I ain't getting involved," Jimmy said. "If I start asking the wrong questions, I might never make it out of Cleveland alive."

Jimmy left Ahern's office knowing that all he did, concerning the Cleveland mob's problems, was recommend Ray Ferritto for a little work on the side. But at this point, Jimmy was sorry he had gotten involved even to that extent.

People rat when they're facing big time in the can. Jimmy hoped Cleveland's gang problems, concerning Danny Greene, were worked out in Cleveland without Ray Ferritto's involvement.

Unfortunately, that turned out not to be the case.

Two days after his meeting with Ahern, Jimmy flew to Cleveland with his right hand man, Mike Rizzi (Rizzitello). They met Blackie Licavoli for dinner at a quiet little seafood restaurant in West Milton, Ohio just outside Dayton and 225 miles from Cleveland. To a casual observer, the mobsters looked like upstanding businessmen out for a quiet little chat along with their lobster bisque.

While sipping his soup, Jimmy asked Licavoli, "Have you heard anything else from the FBI broad yet?"

"Nothing yet," Licavoli said. "Like I told you before, it might take some time."

"Okay, keep me posted," Jimmy said. "I'll even chip in a few bucks to pay this broad off right."

"That's not necessary," Licavoli said. "We're taking care of her better than she deserves."

When Jimmy got back to the West Coast, he was in phone contact with Ahern almost every day. The only thing interesting Jimmy found out back in San Francisco, and it was Mike Rizzi that told him, was that Brooklier wanted Jimmy to go over to San Diego and take over Frank Bompensiero's rackets.

"They must think I'm fucking stupid," Jimmy told Ahern. "I go out to San Diego and I'm a sitting duck."

"You're a sitting duck in San Francisco too," Ahern said. "We got word from one of our informants that Tony "The Ant" Spilotro from Chicago is on your case."

"I fucking believe it," Jimmy said. "That cocksucker Joey Aiuppa had Sam Giancana whacked, and he had Johnny Roselli whacked too. He even questioned me about it; asking me how I felt that my two old friends were dead. I played it smart, and said that was just part of the business. But I could tell by the way he was looking at me that he didn't believe a thing I said."

"Jimmy don't get mad at me, but this is what I heard," Ahern said. "The only guy who is close enough to hurt you is Mike Rizzitello. The word is out that he's in on the contract too. Look at it this way, he eliminates you and he moves up a slot in the organization."

Jimmy thought over the possibility of Rizzo changing sides, and it made perfect sense. In the mob, it's always your closest friend who whacks you.

On October 6, 1977, Jimmy got the news that the Cleveland mob finally got rid of Danny Greene. Greene was killed the same way his partner Nardi was – a bomb was planted in a car next to Green's parked car at the Brainard Medical Center. When Green returned to his car, the bomb went boob, and Danny Greene was eliminated as an obstacle to the Cleveland underworld. Jimmy wondered if Ray Ferritto had been involved in Greene's murder. Because if he had been involved and was caught, it was not a stretch to think that Ferritto would point the finger at Jimmy to get a reduction in his prison sentence.

But right now Jimmy had more important problems, closer to home.

As far as Brooklier was concerned, Jimmy decided to take the bull by the horns. He tried repeatedly to contact Brooklier to arrange another sitdown. But Brooklier had stopped taking Jimmy's calls. He was always "not available," or "sick in bed."

Jimmy phoned Louie Dragna and asked him to intercede between him and Brooklier, but Dragna played dumb.

"Jimmy, I'll try to talk with Brooklier," Dragna said. "But the FBI is up my ass. They're watching every move I make."

Being stymied in all directions, Jimmy decided to lay all his cards out on the table. He phoned Tony Brooklier, Dominick's son and attorney.

"Listen Tony, I'm tired of this bullshit about your father refusing to talk to me," Jimmy said. "If this doesn't get straightened out soon, tell your father he'll be facing a grand jury."

"What do you mean about a grand jury?" Tony Brooklier said. "You're talking out of your asshole."

"Yeah, maybe I am," Jimmy said. "But you tell your old man I'm tired of playing his games. You're a lawyer. Figure it out. But one thing's for sure, this is the last time I'll contact any of you motherfuckers. Set up a meeting between me and your old man in a public place. You got my number; you call me. Otherwise, all you son-of-a-bitches will be sorry you ever fucked with Jimmy Fratianno."

Knowing Rizzi might be turning against him, Jimmy sent him to see Russell Bufalino, the crime boss of Northeastern Pennsylvania and a friend of Fratianno's for 40 years. Jimmy wanted to feel things out, see what Bufalino, a boss himself, was thinking about Jimmy's situation.

When Rizzi returned to San Francisco, he told Jimmy things he didn't want to hear, but what he totally expected.

"Russell sends his regards, and he said he's sorry to her about our problems," Rizzi said.

"What do you mean 'by our problems?'?" Jimmy said.

"Well, Russell knows I'm with you," Rizzi said. "Russell said your best bet is to go to Chicago and straighten everything out with Joey Aiuppa."

"That's bullshit and Russell knows that," Jimmy said. "He's trying to lay a trap for me. If I go to Chicago, those mutts will make me disappear."

Rizzi's message from Bufalino confirmed to Jimmy what he had expected. He knew that Bufalino was just laying out the party line. Bosses stick together, and Brooklier, even though Jimmy thought he was a useless bastard, was still a boss. Hell, now Jimmy didn't even trust Blackie Licavoli, who Jimmy had known since they were teenagers.

Jimmy could sense Rizzi was getting cagy, but it clinched the deal in Jimmy's mind that Rizzi was no longer his pal, when Rizzi said, "What did you men when you said they were laying a trap?"

"Don't worry about it, Mike," Jimmy said. "None of these guys in Los Angeles are cagy enough or tough enough to take me down. I'll be the one who does the talking down. Believe me."

Jimmy's feeling about Chicago were confirmed when he got a phone call from his old mob buddy, Marshal Caifano. Caifano said it was very important for Jimmy to get on the next flight to Chicago to see Joe Aiuppa. The reason Caifano gave Jimmy was that Aiuppa wanted Jimmy to introduce him to the "Cowboy," Las Vegas gambling czar Benny Binion.

"Who the fuck are you kidding?" Jimmy told Caifano. "You know Binion as well as I do. Why don't you make the introductions?"

Caifano mumbled something about Aiuppa having strange ways, and that he was just following orders.

"Let's cut the bullshit," Jimmy said. "If you want to see me, come out to San Francisco and we'll talk. Otherwise, go fuck yourself!"

Then he banged down the phone.

Well, that was that. Jimmy knew every mob boss in America wanted Jimmy dead. Brooklier had lied all along about Jimmy's actions while Brooklier was in jail, and he set a trap that Jimmy had no way of escaping. Jimmy knew, sooner or later, he was going to get a bullet in the head.

On November 17, 1977, Jimmy got that telltale phone call from Mike Rizzi.

"We've got to talk," Rizzi had said.

"So talk," Jimmy said. "Who's stopping you?"

"No, this is important stuff, I can't discuss on the phone," Rizzi said. "I'm at a phone booth in Los Angeles. Go to a pay phone right away. You know the one. I'll call you there."

"Mike, there's no fuckin' way I'm leaving the house tonight," Jimmy said. "Call me in a few days."

"This can't wait a few days."

"Then it's too fuckin' bad," Jimmy said.

"Okay, have it your way, Jimmy," Rizzi said.

"Fuck you, Mike," Jimmy said.

And he banged the phone back into its cradle.

The next day Jimmy found out from Ahern that Rizzi had made that phone call from a phone booth one quarter of a mile from Jimmy's house.

There was no turning back now; Jimmy "The Weasel" Fratianno decided to make the best of a bad situation. Not trusting anyone in the mob, Jimmy decided to use his ace in the hole - the Witness Protection Program - which had been pitched to him by Ahern from the moment they had met.

Jimmy dialed Ahern's phone number.

"Look, I'm moving out of my apartment, and going into hiding for a while," Jimmy told Ahern.

"What about your wife, Jean?" Ahern said.

"Don't worry about her," Jimmy said. "She with her family in San Pedro."

"Jimmy, I don't want to scare you, but things are happening fast," Ahern said. "We need to talk right away."

"Well, I moving today, and I should be settled by tomorrow," Jimmy said.

"Okay, meet me at the Holiday Inn at the airport," Ahern said. "At two in afternoon tomorrow. I'll be in room 222."

Jimmy arrived his customary 20 minutes late, and he was stunned that room 222 was stuffed with FBI agents. As soon as Jimmy closed the door behind him, Ahern stood up and began reading Jimmy his rights, while four agents handcuffed Jimmy behind his back.

"What the fuck is going on here?" Jimmy said.

"Jimmy, I'm arresting you for murder," Ahern said.

"Who's murder, what the fuck are you talking about?" Jimmy said.

"Ray Ferritto was arrested and he implicated several people in the murder of Danny Greene, including you," Ahern said.

"That's bullshit," Jimmy said. "I was here in San Francisco when Greene was murdered."

"Jimmy you've been around for a while; I don't have to explain the law to you," Ahern said. "You don't have to make the bomb or pull the switch to be charged with murder. The Cleveland police say they have enough evidence to charge you with conspiracy to commit murder."

"And I say they don't?" Jimmy said. "So let's go to Cleveland and find out."

"Look Jimmy, I can help you out a lot here," Ahern said. "But you got to tell us the truth. I want to know everything that happened here on the West Coast since you arrived. I want to know the whole story about Frank Bompensiero's murder. We know the people involved were Ricciardi, Rizzi, Brooklier and Sciortino. We just need you to fill in the gaps. You play ball with us, and I'll see what I can do for you in Cleveland."

At this point, Jimmy figured there was no downside to cooperating with the feds. He was facing a murder change in Cleveland, and by singing the right tune, Jimmy could obtain a huge break in sentencing, plus gain revenge against Brooklier and his cohorts as an added benefit.

"Okay, here goes," Jimmy said. "You better have a tape recorder rolling, because I can give you the entire Los Angeles mob bosses in one fell swoop. But I want immunity and protection."

"I'll do what I can for you, Jimmy. I promise you that," Ahern said. "But If I catch you in just one lie, the deal is off."

Jimmy asked that his cuffs be removed so he could smoke one of his big cigars. Ahern relented, figuring a loose and relaxed Jimmy Fratianno was the best and the quickest way to loosen his tongue.

"Okay, this is how the Bomp deal went down," Jimmy said. "Brooklier got Bomp to the phone. Ricciardi was the shooter, and Lo Cicero was the getaway driver. And Louie Dragna was in on the planning from the beginning. It took almost two fucking years to clip Bomp."

"You're right," Jimmy Ahern said. "Those are the big boys for sure on the West Coast. Now I have a shitload more questions for you. Are you up to the task?"

"Shit yeah," Jimmy said. "Considering the circumstances, this could be a lot of fun."

As park of Jimmy's plea deal with the feds, he would have to plead guilty to conspiracy in the murder of Danny Greene, and he would have to divulge every murder he committed himself, or was in on the conspiracy. Secondly, Jimmy had to agree to testify in whatever trials the feds thought he could be a valuable witness. If Jimmy did all the feds asked, he would be given a sentence of five years, with the possibility of parole in just 21 months (which is exactly what Jimmy got in jail – 21 months, almost all of it in country club settlings like the Valachi suite in La Tuna, Texas.)

To Jimmy, the deal seemed too good to be true.

"I was told never to look a gift horse in the mouth," Jimmy told the feds. "So let's get the ball rolling on my deal."

As a result of Jimmy's cooperation and his uncanny knack of remembering the exact details of crimes committed decades decades ago, top mob bosses from coast to coast were thrust into the fire without sizzling in the fry pan first.

The first case Jimmy testified in was the Westchester Premier Theater case, in which nine defendants were accused of violating security laws and robbing the theater until it was forced to claim bankruptcy. As a result of Jimmy testimony, the theater's owner of record, Eliot Weisman, got six years in prison, mobster Greg DePalma got 54 months, Richie "Nerves" Fusco got 30 months, and Frank Sinatra's pal, Louie "Dome" Pacella, got a mere two years. Fringe mobster and stockbroker, Salvatore Cannatella, got one year and one day. And Tommy Marson, the man who brought Jimmy into the deal, also got one year and one day. Four other men were found not guilty, including Gambino captain, Nino Gaggi.

In the next ten years, besides the trials of the West Coast mob, Jimmy testified in dozen of mob trials, including those of Cleveland's Blackie Licavoli, New York City Gambino captain, Aniello Dellacroce, and Chicago mobster, Marshall Caifano – all of whom were found guilty. In 1981, Jimmy also testified in the RICO trial of Genovese crime family boss, Funzi Tieri. Tieri was found guilty and was sentenced to ten years in prison. However, Tieri died two months later of natural cause at the Mount Sinai Hospital in New York.

All in all, during the next 10 years, Jimmy's testimony put 26 mobsters in jail, including Columbo crime family boss, Carmine Persico, whom Jimmy had never met.

To show he was a "Weasel" to the end, after he did his 21 months in prison, Jimmy Fratianno demanded and got from the government payments as high as $50,000 for testifying in certain cases. He also made some serious coin from the publishing of not one, but two autobiographies of the man himself. A few years after *The Last Mafioso* ,written by Ovid Demaris, was published in 1981, Jimmy claimed Demaris got major parts of the book all wrong. As a result, Jimmy was able to get writer Michael J. Zuckerman to write a second bio called *Vengeance is Mine*.

In 1982, Jimmy was paid $250 an hour for his preparation and testimony in a $630 million defamation of character suit file by the luxurious California resort Rancho La Costa against Bob Guccione and *Penthouse Magazine*. In 1975, *Penthouse* had run an article entitled "La Costa: The Hundred Million Dollar Resort with Criminal Clientele." Jimmy, who was hired by *Penthouse* lawyer Roy Grutman, testified that he and many other mobsters, including Moe Dalitz, the mob boss of Cleveland, had spent many quality weeks at this famous resort. As a result of Jimmy's testimony *Penthouse* prevailed, and Rancho La Costa went home with its tail between its legs, minus the settlement money, and minus millions of dollars in attorney's fees. For his trouble, merely a couple of weeks' work, Jimmy pocketed a cool $40,000.

In 1987, the government got tired of Jimmy "The Weasel" and his continuous shakedowns of the government for money, and more money, in order for him to "tell the truth" on the witness stands.

Justice Department spokesman, James Donovan, said, "We think Mr. Fratianno has given invaluable service to the government and law enforcement. But the Witness Protection Program is set up to protect people; not to reward them."

The government reported that in a ten-year period they had given Jimmy almost $1 million ($951,326) to cover "housing, utilities, food, and other expenses." Those other expenses included his wife, Jean's, extravagant spending sprees on furniture, jewelry and clothing, as well as auto (2 cars) and household insurance and real estate taxes for two homes and a condominium.

At one point, according to a government source, Fratianno even sought federal reimbursement for the cleaning and glazing of his wife's mink jackets and the cost of her nicotine withdrawal treatments. Thankfully, those requests were turned down.

After the FBI gave Jimmy the boot, Jimmy appealed to the Justice Department, claiming that his testimony had been invaluable for the government in high profile mob cases and would continue to be valuable in the future.

The Justice Department denied Jimmy's appeal, saying, "Any further payments to Mr. Fratianno might make the program appear to be a 'pension fund for aging mobsters.'"

Incensed, Jimmy agreed to appear on ABC's "Good Morning America." Jimmy's figure was blacked out on television, to protect his identity.

"Government prosecutors don't care," Fratianno told the morning national television audience. "I would advise anybody to think twice before they go on this program, because, after they're through using you, they throw you out in the street. I'm just washed up now, you know. I'd like to feel secure at this stage of the game."

Fratianno said that the mob still has a $250,000 contract on his life, and that the government's actions left him "a dead man."

Fratianno also said, "I put 30 guys away, six of them bosses, and now the whole world's looking for me."

Fratianno, who had recently been on the Oprah Winfrey Show to plug his new book, *Vengeance is Mine*, a book he has never read (he never read *The Last Mafioso* either), said, "If the book sells, then I'll have some money and I can go someplace, leave the country. That's what I want to do. I hope and pray nobody finds me because they don't forget. After I got out of prison, I went in the Witness Protection Program with my wife. The mob found out where I was at, and I had a very close call in Boise, Idaho. They found me, but I spotted them first and I left."

Jimmy spent the rest of his life on the run from the mob, mostly out of the country in places like the Dominican Republican and Costa Rica.

On June 30, 1993, Jimmy "The Weasel" Fratianno, 79, bought the ranch in an undisclosed location. A spokesman for the Federal Bureau of Investigation in Phoenix, Jack Callahan, said in a telephone interview with the *New York Times* that Mr. Fratianno had "died peacefully in his sleep."

His wife, Jean, told the *Los Angeles Times* that her husband, who was suffering from Alzheimer's disease, died at their home in an undisclosed United States location while living under an assumed name. He had previously suffered a series of strokes.

The wicked and convoluted life of Jimmy "The Weasel" Fratianno, who became the highest-paid participant in the history of the Witness Protection Program, was best summed up by Nick Ackerman, a former assistant U.S. attorney in Manhattan who prosecuted one of the Mafia cases in which Fratianno testified.

"He basically is who he is," Ackerman said. "If you called over to Central Casting and asked for a guy to play a mob boss, he'd be the perfect guy."

It is after blowing the Two Tonys' brains out that Jimmy Fratianno ponders the passing of it all: "There ain't too many guys in our thing these days that can do this kind of work," Jack (Dragna) had told him. "In the old days, you had to prove yourself. Now it's all different. If you've got fifteen percent that are killers, you're lucky. Take Chicago, they've got maybe three hundred guys and if they've got thirty killers, that's tops. Most guys just ain't got the stomach for it. Know what I mean, they're squeamish. I can't figure them out."

*****

What people are saying about "Jimmy "The Weasel" Fratianno –

5.0 out of 5 stars

Great Fun Read!

By Curfewplug

I've read hundreds of books about organized crime; some good, some not so good. This was one of my favorites. I enjoy Mr. Bruno's writing style, lively, informative, and just the right amount of street jargon.

5.0 out of 5 stars

JOE BRUNO, YOU'VE DONE IT AGAIN

By Eddie Lazinsky

Great read!! I just couldn't put it down. The pages just flowed. Keep up the good work Joe. I'm looking forward to reading more of your books

5.0 out of 5 stars

Great read!!

By lcook0825

As usual a great read involving the Mafia in NYC. Very well written and I finished in one sitting. Lots of research goes into Joes books and it just keeps you reading. I'm looking forward to his next one as I always do.

5.0 out of 5 stars

Excellent read, thank you Joe Bruno!!

By Chester L. Stone

When I see a Joe Bruno title I expect to be entertained and educated and "Jimmy 'The Weasel' Fratianno" fills that expectation. Joe Bruno is a combination of a historian, crime reporter and educator. As I have said before reading Joe Bruno is like having a conversation with an old friend.

What People Are Saying About Joe Bruno's Books:

ANOTHER HISTORY LESSON! – I love Joe Bruno's books. I always say that he's the NYC true crime historian. NYC has had its share of murder and corruption over the past couple of centuries and the author is a wealth of knowledge about it. A must read for any true crime book collector. - RJ Parker - Best Selling Author of True Crime Books

TRUE CRIME AT ITS BEST!! - Joe Bruno has a way of giving real light into his mob stories. His easy writing style pulls you in, and his no BS attitude allows you as a reader to get the full story not just what he chooses to share. There is so much real life history in these books. His books are especially edge of your seat interesting. They are mind blowing, really. I would highly recommend you pick up a copy of one of his books. You'll see what I am talking about. – Brenda Perlin – Adult Contemporary Fiction Author.

INFORMATIVE AND JUST PLAIN GREAT! - I love reading about mobsters and old New York. Joe Bruno is an awesome author. I highly recommend Joe Bruno's books. – Patricia Epps

KNOCK OUT PUNCH! - Joe Bruno delivers a hard punch, well researched, no nonsense book. Fear, hatred, and brutality bring to our awareness in a most convincing and stark manner. The reader is an observer as chills run up and down the spine. Joe Bruno brings full realism to play and bear upon our psyches - Joyce Metzger

Bibliography

The May, 16, 1977 issue of Time Magazine

A Bad, Bad, Boy – The Most Feared Mobster in California in 30 Years by Judith Moore, Jim Holman and Sandy Huffake

The Mammoth Book of the Mafia – Nigel Hawthorne – Robinson Press, 2009

The Los Angeles Times

Mickey Cohen: The Life and Crimes of L.A.'s Notorious Mobster
By Tere Tereba

His Way: The Unauthorized Biography of Frank Sinatra
By Kitty Kelley

California Case Law -People v. Fratianno
132 Cal. App. 2d 610
paperlessarchives.com - The Lucille Ball- Desi Arnaz files –

Mickey Cohen, My Own Words